INVITING STUDENTS TO

100

TIPS FOR TALKING
EFFECTIVELY
WITH YOUR STUDENTS

JENNY EDWARDS

INVITING STUDENTS TO LEARN

100 TIPS FOR TALKING EFFECTIVELY WITH YOUR STUDENTS

ASCD

Alexandria, Virginia USA

1703 N. Beauregard St. • Alexandria, VA 22311-1714 USA
Phone: 800-933-2723 or 703-578-9600 • Fax: 703-575-5400
Web site: www.ascd.org • E-mail: member@ascd.org
Author guidelines: www.ascd.org/write

Gene R. Carter, *Executive Director;* Nancy Modrak, *Publisher;* Scott Willis, *Director, Book Acquisitions & Development;* Carolyn Pool, *Acquisitions Editor;* Julie Houtz, *Director, Book Editing & Production;* Leah Lakins, *Editor;* Georgia Park, *Senior Graphic Designer;* Mike Kalyan, *Production Manager;* Carmen Yuhas, *Production Specialist;* Marlene Hochberg, *Typesetter*

PAPERBACK ISBN: 978-1-4166-0903-2 ASCD product # 110015 n1/10

Also available as an e-book (see Books in Print for the ISBNs).

Quantity discounts for the paperback edition only: 10–49 copies, 10%; 50+ copies, 15%; for 1,000 or more copies, call 800-933-2723, ext. 5634, or 703-575-5634. For desk copies: member@ascd.org.

Library of Congress Cataloging-in-Publication Data

Edwards, Jenny, 1949-
 Inviting students to learn : 100 tips for talking effectively with your students / Jenny Edwards.
   p. cm.
 Includes bibliographical references and index.
 ISBN 978-1-4166-0903-2 (pbk. : alk. paper)
 1. Communication in education. 2. Motivation in education. 3. Teacher-student relationships. I. Title.
 LB1033.5.E39 2010
 371.102'2–dc22
                          2009038224

20 19 18 17 16 15 14 13 12 11 10   1 2 3 4 5 6 7 8 9 10 11 12

INVITING STUDENTS TO
LEARN

100 TIPS FOR TALKING EFFECTIVELY WITH YOUR STUDENTS

Acknowledgments

I owe a debt of gratitude to many people:

To my wonderful husband, Bo, who encouraged me to pursue my dreams;

To my parents, Tom and Evelyn Ingle, who taught me the value of continuous learning;

To Chris Hall, who gave me incredible insights into language;

To Art Costa and Bob Garmston, who developed Cognitive Coaching and greatly encouraged me;

To Bruce Wellman, who taught me precision in language;

To Michael Grinder, who taught me fascinating things about nonverbal communication;

To Jim Fay, who first believed in me;

To John Grinder and Richard Bandler, who developed the field of neuro-linguistic programming, and to Milton Erickson and Virginia Satir, who created the work that serves as a base for this field;

To Robert Dilts and Judith DeLozier, who greatly advanced that field;

To my many guides in neuro-linguistic programming (Connierae and Steve Andreas, Laura Ewing, Charles Faulkner, Robert McDonald, Suzy Smith, Tim Hallbom, Gerry Schmidt, and others), who taught me the fine points of using language;

To William Watson Purkey, John Novak, Tommie Radd, Betty Siegel, and Jack Schmidt, who taught me about creating an invitational atmosphere in schools;

To Mark Hochwender, who encouraged me to shoot for the stars;

To Evelyn Mooney, who introduced me to teaching;

To Luis González, who modeled excellence in writing books;

To Michael Dolcemascolo, Kitty Kelly Epstein, Sarah Spilman Geer, Sandie Godsman, Sue Gordon, Susan Johnson, Brooke Kerns, Kass Larsen, Sonia Maldonado, Marsha Manning, Laura Mitchell, Rena Palloff, Heather Sweeney, Judy Witt, Connie Youngblood, and Diane Zimmerman for providing inspiration;

To Leah Lakins and Carolyn Pool at ASCD for their meticulous editing; and to Genny Ostertag and Scott Willis at ASCD for their support.

This book is dedicated to you.

Foreword

F or innumerable reasons, *Inviting Students to Learn* is an amazing
book written for anyone who works with learners—at any age
and at any level. One of the most remarkable capacities of human
beings, particularly young ones, is their capacity to learn language.
Children at only 18 months can already distinguish between "take
this to Daddy" and "bring that to Grandpa." They learn to decode
the syntax of the language they hear and act accordingly.

The language children hear during their formative years has
such a powerful impact on their lives. It affects their self-esteem,
their trust of others, their thinking capacities, their emotional well-
being, their sense of efficacy, their positive or negative attitudes,
and their autonomy, among other things. Jenny Edwards's vast array
of practical suggestions takes advantage of that fact. She notes that
through interactions with responsive, respectful adults, children
learn to imitate and then internalize valued social, physical, cognitive, and ethical behaviors.

Children produce and generate language that is both a product
of their environment and an imitation of the language that they have
heard and interpreted from others. Language is a reflection of people's view of themselves, their styles and beliefs, their perceptions
of the world, and their own thinking. Language refinement plays a

critical role in enhancing a person's ability to think critically, which is the knowledge base for efficacious action.

The language used in everyday interaction with children can actually transform their brains and produce altered behavior affecting their self-knowledge and self-esteem, as well as their beliefs and their willingness to work successfully toward goals. Readers will gather practical, exciting, transformative, and simple-to-employ tips that will help with building relationships with students, teaching, assisting students in planning for the future, responding to student objections, encouraging learning, influencing students, and resolving conflicts.

Enriching the complexity and specificity of language also produces effective thinking. Noted Israeli psychologist Reuven Feuerstein (2000) states: "One of the most interesting and exciting aspects . . . is that the quality of interaction not only changes the structure of behavior of the individual, not only changes the amount and quality of his repertoire, but . . . changes the structure and functioning of the brain itself in very meaningful ways" (p. 275). Our guess is that the material in this book may be as enriching for teachers in these ways as it is for students.

Language and thinking are closely entwined. Like two sides of the same coin, they are inseparable. Fuzzy language is a reflection of fuzzy thinking. Efficacious people strive to communicate accurately in both written and oral form, use precise language, define terms, use correct names, and provide universal labels and analogies. They strive to avoid overgeneralizations, deletions, and distortions, instead supporting their statements with explanations, comparisons, quantification, and evidence.

This brings us to some more of the intriguing ideas contained in this book. Teachers who desire to foster students' positive esteem, encourage them to think critically and creatively, establish a trusting classroom environment, help students enjoy learning, and promote harmonious and reciprocal interactions with others can achieve these results by choosing their language with care, intentionality, and a positive regard for children. Edwards supplies many practical

and profound, simple and powerful, and obvious but subtle suggestions and tips you can use to refine the language you employ in your
everyday interactions with others.

It is amazing to find such a rich compendium of practical knowledge and tips in one book. What's also amazing is that we haven't
learned this before. Why haven't teacher education courses, staff
developers, and teacher leaders employed, modeled, and taught
this valuable information to new and practicing educators?

You are invited to monitor your language as you interact with
others. Choose your language with positive intentions and pay
attention to the influence you have on others—students, parents,
colleagues, and family members—and note how they respond to
your new patterns of discourse. The results will amaze you.

Arthur L. Costa, EdD, Granite Bay, California
Robert J. Garmston, EdD, El Dorado Hills, California

Preface

In striving to excel in any situation, we are aided in our goal by focusing on our higher purposes. What were some of the reasons that you decided to enter the teaching profession? What higher purposes did you want to serve? What led you to choose to teach students at a particular age?

We know one thing for sure—you certainly did not decide to enter the teaching profession for the money! You wanted something more. Perhaps you have wanted to teach since you first played "school" with your friends when you were very small. Perhaps you wanted to make learning experiences better for students than they were for you. Perhaps you wanted to have an impact on the next generation. Perhaps you wanted to instill some of your values in your students. Perhaps you were so excited by what you knew (subject matter, pedagogy, educational psychology, etc.) that you wanted to share it with others to help them develop the same love and appreciation for it that you have.

Whatever the reasons that you decided to enter the field of teaching, you were serving your higher purposes. These language tips are offered in that spirit—to help you achieve your higher purposes in educating students even more powerfully, no matter who your students are or how old they may be. None of us were born knowing how to speak in ways that encourage students. Some of us learned productive language patterns from our parents and teachers; others of us were not as fortunate. As much as our parents loved us, we may have grown up listening to words and messages that were less than empowering.

Inviting Students to Learn is written for anyone who works with learners at any level, including educators, parents, and trainers. In the following chapters, you will find tips for assisting you in what you are already doing—building affirming relationships with students to help them achieve at high levels. While many of these suggested practices may already be in your repertoire, many may be new to you. You can apply the concepts to increase rapport with students and encourage them to work toward their goals in order to serve their own higher purposes. After all, our greatest leverage point is our relationships with our students . . . and they don't cost anything.

In the Introduction, you will find information about the reasons for using language to create invitational classrooms. You will also learn about the importance of expressing caring in schools, modeling effective communication skills, altering students' perceptions, inviting students to learn, and the principles upon which this book is based.

The first chapter focuses on developing a mind-set for communicating invitationally with students. Our words flow out of what is in our hearts and minds. Thinking positive thoughts about students allows us to truly affirm and encourage them. In this chapter, you will learn strategies for valuing students, thinking positive about students, smiling, asking yourself key questions as you are working with students, and focusing on students' positive intentions. You will also learn strategies for building rapport with students and using different voice intonations with them, depending on your purposes for communicating. Other topics include helping students to breathe, managing the classroom, exploring metaphors, and aligning with students' belief systems.

The second chapter contains some of the arenas in which the language tips can be applied, including giving feedback to students; interacting with parents; writing positive notes to students, parents, and colleagues; making positive phone calls; creating positive signs; writing report cards; designing the syllabus; and using technology.

In the third chapter, you will find suggestions for using the book's language tips with diverse groups of students. Of course, you are the expert on what might work for your students. Suggestions are offered for using the tips with special needs students, diverse populations of students, various ages of students, and students in the online environment.

The fourth chapter explores the purposes of using the language tips. They can be used for building relationships with students, teaching, helping students plan for the future, responding to student objections, encouraging students, influencing students, and resolving conflicts.

The fifth chapter is the heart of the book. It comprises 100 tips for talking with students, listed in alphabetical order. A brief rationale for each tip is followed by examples of using the tip with different ages of students.

The ideas in this book are designed to make teaching even more enjoyable for you and your students. As you are developing a mind-set for communicating invitationally with your students, applying the language tips in various arenas, using the language tips with various types of students, and consciously using the tips for different purposes, hopefully, you will discover a renewed sense of joy in teaching. You might even find yourself using the language tips when talking with your friends and family members.

Introduction

The Commission on the Whole Child (2007) emphasized the importance of educators focusing on the whole child in order to assist all children to "develop all of their gifts and realize their full potential" (p. 7), rather than working solely on academic achievement. The commission suggested:

> Through interactions with responsive, respectful adults—regardless of their role within a child's life—children learn to imitate, and then internalize, valued social, physical, cognitive, or ethical behaviors. When children believe that the adults around them care about who they are and what they know and what they can do, they are more likely to respond to what those adults value and take those values as their own. (p. 16)

As Gene R. Carter, executive director for ASCD, asked, "If the student were truly at the center of the system, what could we achieve?" (Commission on the Whole Child, 2007, p. 4).

Stories abound of students who succeeded against all odds because teachers or other adults believed in them and expressed that belief both verbally and nonverbally. On the other hand, the news is also filled with stories of adults and children who expressed their anger with violence because they were not affirmed or spoken kindly to as they were growing up.

Werner (1989) studied children on the island of Kauai for 30 years. She found that children who succeeded against all odds had "support networks" outside of their immediate families—people in their lives who helped them to have "a sense of meaning in their lives and a belief that they could control their fate, ... [bringing about] an attitude of hopefulness" (p. 110). Werner concluded that "competence, confidence and caring can flourish even under adverse circumstances if young children encounter people in their lives who provide them with a secure basis for the development of trust, autonomy and initiative" (p. 111). A major goal of the language tips in this book is to enable educators to express caring and support for their students in order to enable and empower students to succeed beyond their wildest dreams.

Negative language surrounds us in newspapers, on television, and in conversations. Take a look at the front section of a daily newspaper, and you will see words such as the following: "fall sharply," "crash," "almost gone," "bans," "destroys," "delays," "criticizes," "debate," "severe," "blame," "weakening," "fading," "illegal," "fighting," "venom," "strikes," and so on. In the media, even when we read a positive statement, it is often immediately followed by the word "but," which tends to cancel out what came before it (Hall, 2004). We continually read about negative possibilities in the future. The authors of the articles don't know for sure, but they want to let us know that dire consequences *may* occur, and it appears that we can't do anything about the situation. With such negativity constantly in the air, it makes sense that we need to be even more intentional when speaking with students. Rather than creating a culture of fear, we want to create a culture of warmth, caring, encouragement, and empowerment.

Jackson (1968) cited that "the [elementary] teacher engages in as many as 1,000 interpersonal interchanges each day" (p. 11). Berliner (1984) discussed the numerous decisions that teachers make every day. One type of decision was "communicating academic expectations for achievement" (p. 66). He suggested, based on the literature, "that there are powerful effects on performance when teachers communicate their goals for performance to those they are teaching" (p. 66). We can communicate those high expectations by carefully selecting the words that we use.

Expressing Caring in Schools

The following poem expresses the focus of this book:

A Language That Expresses Care

We speak with words;

but words are not just uttered,

they are chosen.

We use a language;

but that language is not merely words,

it is a unique way of choosing to be in the world.

We teach others a way of being in the world;

but they are not mere recipients,

they also choose to show us their lives and hopes.
(John Novak in Purkey & Novak, 1996, p. 9; used with permission)

Plato said, "Be kind, for everyone you meet is fighting a hard battle." Think about how this quote applies to the students in your classroom. They are all fighting some battle, whether they are children, teenagers, or adults. How we interact with our students may affect the outcomes of those battles. Lambeth (1980) found that secondary student achievement was related to teacher caring, respect, and other elements of interpersonal relationships.

In the mid-1980s, when I was teaching Jim Fay and Foster Cline's seminar titled "Discipline with Love and Logic," one of their overhead transparencies included a quote from Theodore Roosevelt: "Nobody cares how much you know, until they know how much you care." That struck me as a wonderful motto, and I have carried it with me ever since. Truly, our students don't care how much we know, as teachers and instructors, until they know how much we care about them.

Years ago, the son of a friend had just started 1st grade. I asked him how he liked school. His eyes grew wide, and he had a giant smile on his face. "My teacher *really* likes me!" he exclaimed. I have pondered his comment through the years, visualizing his ecstatic look. As an educator, how can I communicate that I *really* like all of my students? Ladson-Billings (1994) conducted a study in which she investigated the practices of teachers who were effective with African American students. In one classroom, she asked the students:

"What is it that you like about the class?"

"The teacher!" they responded in unison.

"What do you like about the teacher?" I probed.

"She listens to us!"

"She respects us!"

"She lets us express our opinions!"

"She looks us in the eye when she talks to us!"

"She smiles at us!"

"She speaks to us when she sees us in the hall or in the cafeteria!"
(p. 68)

Another teacher in Ladson-Billings's study summed up how we should be treating our students by saying that she treats students as though they were her own children.

Modeling Effective Communication Skills

As we talk with students and with each other, students are assimilating and subsequently modeling our language. We may even affect the ways that families talk with each other as our students use our language at home! Short and colleagues (1999) found that students imitated the language that their teachers used. As a result of conducting their study, they realized the importance of teachers modeling the types of interactions and language that they wanted their students to use.

In the mid-1990s, I managed a million-dollar grant in which teachers were trained in Michael Grinder's (2005) Nonverbal Classroom Management technique. Teachers learned 31 nonverbal strategies that they could use with students. They received coaching first from Michael, and then from colleagues in their schools who were trained to be "Green Chair Coaches." In one of the classrooms that I visited, a student was in charge of the classroom after the lunch period as children came in from the playground. I laughed as I watched the student use the strategies perfectly! Obviously, she was modeling what she had seen her teacher do.

Altering Students' Perceptions

Another goal of the language tips in this book is to help students perceive things in alternate ways. Any given situation can be framed in a number of contexts, each of which can result in quite different feelings. For example, when I go to Denver for my hair appointment, I typically need to park quite a long way from the salon. I have a choice of how I can view the long walk from my car: I can either complain and feel angry, or I can be grateful for the opportunity to get some additional exercise. After all, I pay dues at the gym to be able to use the treadmill!

A friend recently shared a story that shows how even her 5-year-old son had picked up on the concept of perceiving things differently. One day she came home exhausted, lay down on the sofa, and said, "I am feeling tired, sad, and discouraged." Her son immediately countered, "But Mom, you can also look at the situation in lots of other ways!"

When you use the language tips in this book, you may open up new choices for students that they hadn't yet discovered. When we are feeling "stuck," we don't perceive that we have any choices. When we perceive that we have several choices, and that we can choose between them, we gain a new sense of empowerment and energy.

Inviting Students to Learn

The ultimate goal of this book is to help educators send inviting messages to students to help them to realize that they are capable and can learn. According to Purkey and Novak (1996),

> Inviting messages are intended to inform people that they are able, valuable, and responsible; that they have opportunities to participate in their own development; and that they are cordially summoned to take advantage of these opportunities. Conversely, a disinviting message informs its recipients that they are irresponsible, incapable, and worthless and that they cannot participate in activities of any significance. An inviting message is an effort to establish a cooperative interaction; a disinviting message is an effort to establish a controlling or negative interaction. (p. 10)

Each day that we influence the lives of our students, we are also influencing our own. Ladson-Billings (1994) discussed the philosophy of Margaret Rossi, one of the teachers in her study. According to Ladson-Billings, "Rossi understands that her future is inextricably linked with that of her students. By ensuring their success, she reasons, she ensures her own" (p. 89). According to Rossi,

> These children are the future. There is no way for me to have a secure future if they don't have one. It's going to take three of them

to support one of me in my retirement years. They have to be capable of assuming highly skilled positions. (p. 17)

We reap rewards in the present as well. McCombs and Whisler (1997) observed that "learner-centered practices can also make an educator's life more satisfying. Far less energy is needed to devise new ways to keep students involved in class or to make learning interesting to them" (p. 59).

This book is based on the following seven principles:

1. Being intentional in every conversation and choosing words to use with students in order to help them feel strong, thus enabling them to be successful in what they are doing.

2. Stating what we are saying positively.

3. Using words that end with "-ing" to help students make videos in their head and see learning and living as ongoing processes.

4. Intentionally using numerous positive presuppositions— phrases in which we are communicating that the student is highly capable and will be succeeding in many ways, both now and in the future.

5. Assisting students in going into the future and looking back, having already been highly successful in all that they plan on doing.

6. Helping students realize that when they are thinking negative thoughts about their abilities, their thoughts are only perceptions at that moment in time and are subject to change.

7. Letting students know that they have complete choice in the ways that they feel and react in any situation.

The table in Figure 1 (see pp. 153–157) is a handy guide that cross-references the invitational language tips in Chapter 5 with the contexts in which they are most appropriate. You can use this table to help you identify the most appropriate use of the language tips in any situation.

1

Developing a Mind-set for Communicating Invitationally with Students

What do you believe? What do you *really* believe about students, learning, the classroom, your role, and what you would like to accomplish? What do you presuppose about students and learning? Do you believe that students are basically responsible, valuable, and able? Do you believe that educating students is a cooperative, collaborative process, and that your students have untapped potential? Do you believe that all of your students can and will learn? Purkey and Novak (1996) state that those involved in invitational education "work toward developing caring behaviors, nurturing environments, person-centered policies, engaging programs, and democratic processes" (p. 5). They suggest that invitational education is based on five principles:

1. People are able, valuable, and responsible and should be treated accordingly.

2. Educating should be a collaborative, cooperative activity.

3. The process is the product in the making.

4. People possess untapped potential in all areas of worthwhile human endeavor.

5. This potential can best be realized by places, policies, programs, and processes specifically designed to invite development and by people who are intentionally inviting with themselves and others personally and professionally. (p. 3)

Holcomb-McCoy (2000) echoed those beliefs when talking about working with students who are from a different culture from one's own. Her first four preconditions are applicable for teachers. She suggests that multiculturally proficient counselors should

1. Have faith in the students' ability to grow and to fully realize their potential, given responsive, supportive, and developmental intervention across both cultural contexts in which the students are immersed;

2. Examine their own personal attitudes and personality style and how these characteristics influence how they behave with culturally diverse students;

3. Understand that sociopolitical forces influence how culturally diverse students act;

4. Become familiar with the differences in worldviews that characterize ethnic minority students and the implications for counseling. (p. 5)

For a moment, imagine interacting with students with the mind-set that they are broken, filled with problems, and not fun to teach (Hall, 2004). How do you picture these interactions? How might the students react to you? How might it feel to go to work every day with that mind-set?

Now, imagine interacting with students with the mind-set that they are brilliant, geniuses, filled with potential, and fun to teach. How would the quality of such interactions differ? How might students react to you? How might it feel to go to work every day with that mind-set? By believing that students are brilliant and that it is a privilege to have our lives touch their lives, however briefly, we can create a dynamic relationship with them and set the course for communicating invitationally with students.

Teachers need to believe that their students are capable of performing tasks, have value, and can take responsibility for what they need to do (Purkey, 2000). According to Wlodkowski (1984), one strategy that teachers can use to motivate students is to intentionally help them develop a positive attitude toward the teacher, the subject and learning situation, and themselves. Teachers can also help students create an expectation of success.

What do you believe about yourself as a teacher and your ability to have an impact on the lives of the students you teach? Do you believe that you are making a difference? Do you believe that you have the skills to assist students in becoming everything they want to become? Or do you believe that you have little power over the outcomes in your classroom and that the media, the students' home backgrounds, their friends, and other negative influences have more impact on them than you could possibly have?

Purkey (2000) discussed the relationship between what teachers say to students and what students say to themselves. He suggested that the language that teachers use with each other, including their feelings about themselves, their students, their subject matter, and teaching in general, has a powerful impact on their interactions with students, which in turn have a powerful impact on what students say to themselves.

What do you believe about learning? Do you believe that learning is fun and to be enjoyed, or do you believe that learning is drudgery, difficult, and not fun (Hall, 2004)? Do you believe that learning is a reciprocal process and that you learn as much from your students as they learn from you? Do you believe that it is a privilege to be able to come to school every day and work with your students in the natural, enjoyable process of learning?

For a moment, imagine interacting with students with the mind-set that learning is drudgery and hard work. How does that feel? How do you picture students interacting with you? What is the quality of your teaching and their learning?

Now, imagine interacting with students with the mind-set that learning is a natural process that is enjoyable and fun, filled with new discoveries! How does that feel? How do you picture students interacting with you now? What is the quality of your teaching and their learning?

Keep your thoughts positive

Because your thoughts become your words.

Keep your words positive

Because your words become your behaviors.

Keep your behaviors positive

Because your behaviors become your habits.

Keep your habits positive

Because your habits become your values.

Keep your values positive

Because your values become your destiny.

—*Mahatma Gandhi*

This chapter includes information about developing a mind-set for communicating invitationally with students. Information is included about valuing students, thinking positive thoughts about students, the importance of smiling, asking key questions, looking for positive intentions, exploring metaphors, establishing rapport, using intonation, breathing, managing the classroom, and aligning with students' belief systems.

Valuing Students

Students need to know that we value them. By communicating the value we hold for students, we can help them to appreciate themselves and feel powerful and accepted. As a result of our telling them how important they are, they will come to believe that they are important. We will also be building powerful, trusting relationships with them.

One way to communicate students' value is by dressing well. When I moved to a new school and my colleagues were trying to convince me to wear blue jeans and a t-shirt to school, I checked with the principal. He affirmed the value of dressing well to communicate the value of students. Other ways to communicate the esteem we hold for students include the following statements:

- "You are really special, and I feel fortunate to be your teacher this year."
- "You are truly a special class! As you move forward, it will be fun to see all of the exciting and powerful things that you do with your lives for the benefit of many people around the world!"
- "Thank you for being here. It's a joy and a privilege to have the opportunity to work with you!"

Thinking Positive Thoughts About Students

What we think about our students eventually comes out of our mouths. When we think positive thoughts about students, we find ourselves communicating positively with them. If we should happen to think negative thoughts about them, our negative thoughts will eventually come out in our language.

Rosenthal and Jacobson (1992) performed a study in which they told teachers in a school that a certain 20 percent of the students were going to make huge academic gains the following year based on a test that they had taken. In reality, the students had been selected randomly. Sure enough, those students showed significantly more growth in IQ by the end of the school year than students who had not been identified. The researchers called this "the Pygmalion effect"—the teachers who thought positively about their students made their thoughts come true!

In the 1980s, I learned a method to use when talking with a person. I surround that person with positive thoughts, viewing a circle around him or her. As I talk, I consciously think that this is the most wonderful person in the world. After all, that person is taking the time to talk with me!

How many minutes per day do we waste in thinking negative thoughts? If we were to add up the time that we spent during the course of a week, a month, a year, 5 years, 10 years, and a lifetime, we would be astounded at the huge amount of time that we waste in this manner. Hall (personal communication, May 2006) suggested a strategy to use when we find ourselves thinking negative, unproductive thoughts.

The strategy is quite simple. When you have a negative thought, just say, "Thank you." Try it! Bring up some negative thoughts that have been turning over in your mind, whether about an event, yourself, or another person. Now say, "Thank you." Do it again. Bring up those negative thoughts. Now say, "Thank you." Do it several times. What do you notice? The thoughts just fly away, don't they? The more we say "Thank you," the more they stay away.

Ann Lewis, one of the teachers in Ladson-Billings's (1994) study, was asked to take a particularly troubled child in her class. "Other teachers in the school referred to him as 'an accident just waiting to happen.' . . . Lewis referred to Larry as 'a piece of crystal'" (p. 111). Lewis remembered,

> He's strong and beautiful but fragile. I have to build a safe and secure place for him and let him know that we—the class and I—will be here for him. The school has been placing him in the kitchen junk drawer. I want him to be up there in the china cabinet where everyone can see him. (p. 111)

How would our world be different if we put all of our students up there in the china cabinet where everyone could see them?

Smiling

Can you remember a time when someone's smile made a huge difference and changed your mood? The first time that I went on an airplane when I was 13 years old, I felt scared. I didn't know what to expect. Was I going to be safe? I happened to look out the window on the other side of the plane. I caught the eye of the woman sitting there, and she smiled at me. I can still see her smile. Somehow, by smiling, she was telling me that everything was going to be all right. I have loved flying ever since then and can still remember the impact of her smile!

Even when we work with students at a distance, we can smile over the phone. They can still hear the smile in our voices and detect our warmth. By smiling as we are talking, we convey to them that they are important.

In addition, when we call parents to discuss various things with them, they can hear our smiles in the way we talk with them. The more we smile, the happier we become, and the happier we make others around us—including our students!

Asking Key Questions

Leslie Cameron-Bandler (J. Grinder, personal communication, June 1993) suggested that people automatically ask themselves certain questions as they go about their daily life. We may ask ourselves one set of questions when we are in the classroom working with students and another set of questions in our personal lives. We may ask ourselves the same question or set of questions in all contexts of our lives. The questions that we ask ourselves powerfully influence what we say both to ourselves and to students.

When I learned this concept at a training, I was preparing to give a seminar in a school district. I pondered my key question and realized that all my life, I had asked myself, "Will people like me?" I brainstormed various alternative key questions, wondering what key questions would specifically apply to the group of educators with whom I would be working. I had just completed my dissertation on Cognitive Coaching[SM] (Edwards, 1993), and the superintendent of the school district had invited me to work with the people in his district to help design a study to investigate their outcomes from using the program. I knew that I was qualified to help them get what they wanted—results that would enable them to get continued funding for Cognitive Coaching. I decided to use the key question, "How can I be of service to them and help them get what they want?"

As I presented the seminar, I played a game in my mind. Every time that the question, "Will they like me?" came up, I replaced it with, "How can I be of service to them and help them get what they want?" I engaged in this mental game a number of times throughout the day, always smiling to myself.

When the superintendent's wife took me to the airport, she said, "You know, Charlie paid you a compliment." I asked what it was. She said, "Charlie said, 'You know, Jenny just wants to help us!'" Wow! If my key question had come through so powerfully during the seminar, what had people experienced when they interacted with me prior to my learning this concept?

When we ask ourselves questions that can only be answered with "yes" or "no," we can create a negative situation for ourselves. Some examples of those types of questions follow:

- "Will I be successful?"
- "Can I learn to do this?"
- "Will people like me?"
- "Am I okay?"
- "Am I smart enough?"

Open-ended questions that can be answered in many different positive ways are more productive:

- "How can I help all of my students learn today?"
- "In what ways can I be of service to everyone I meet today?"
- "How can I leave the people I meet today feeling better than when I first met them?"
- "How can I make learning fun for my students today?"
- "How can I help every student in my classroom to feel successful today?"

We can also share the concept of key questions with our students so they become conscious of the questions they ask themselves. Successful students might ask key questions such as these:

- "How can I do well today?"
- "How can I learn everything that I possibly can learn today?"
- "What can I do to make even more friends today?"
- "How can I make today a wonderful day?"
- "How can I accomplish everything that I possibly can today?"
- "What are some things that I can do today to move even closer toward achieving my goals?"

Looking for Positive Intentions

People generally have positive intentions (Andreas & Faulkner, 1994). By being curious about the positive intentions that students might have, we can speak kind and affirming words to them and be gentle with them. For example, what might be some of the positive intentions behind procrastinating? Students might procrastinate because their top priority is caring for a sick mother or a sick child; they might not know how to do the assignment and don't want to bother the teacher; or they might be concerned that their skills are not good enough.

If a student hits another student, although it should not happen, we can look for the positive intentions behind it. What might be some positive intentions? The student who was hit might have hurt the self-esteem of the first student or insulted his or her mother or sibling. The student doing the hitting might have seen his or her mother being hit the night before and simply modeled the behavior. The student doing the hitting might be calling for help from the teacher. Flicker and Hoffman (2006) suggested that before punishing a student or using a particular behavior management strategy for misbehavior, teachers should examine numerous possible causes for the behavior and then act in the best interests of the student.

Wellman (personal communication, September 1995) once told me that he never judged the actions of people who were in his training until he had brainstormed at least 20 reasons for their actions. He looked for positive intentions behind their actions. In a Cognitive Coaching training for our school district for a group of more than 100 teachers, participants at a table in the back of the room were talking while he was presenting. I thought that this was rude. He gestured toward their table, and they continued to talk. Not wanting to embarrass them, yet concerned that their talking might interfere with the learning of people at other tables, he asked people to turn to their neighbors and discuss what they were learning so that he could find out what was happening. It turned out that a woman who was nine months pregnant had not wanted to miss the training that day, and she was experiencing contractions. Instead of going to the hospital to have her baby, she had chosen to come to the training because she valued it and really wanted to learn. The people at her table were timing her contractions so that she could drive to the hospital in time to have her baby. As this example illustrates, it can be beneficial to assume that learners have positive intentions and talk with them from that viewpoint, expressing care and concern and searching for the positive intentions behind their actions.

Even if students are not behaving as we would prefer, we can complement the positive intention behind their behavior. For example, if you have difficulty getting students to come back together after a work period, you might say, "It appears as though everyone is really excited about the material" or "It looks like you are really enjoying talking with your friends." If a student has not handed in an assignment, you could say, "You really have a full life with lots of things to do." If students don't come right away when we call them in from recess, you might say, "It's good to see you enjoying exercising and being with your friends." By valuing students' positive intentions, we convey the message that we value them, as well.

Exploring Metaphors

All people have metaphors for living and metaphors for learning, whether they are aware of them or not.

Metaphors for Living

According to Faulkner (1991), each of us has a different metaphor for living. The metaphors that we subscribe to also influence the language that we use with ourselves and with students. In his tapes, Faulkner mentioned the following metaphors used by individuals:

- *Life is a garden.* This person, if a woman, might have flowers on her clothes, in her house, in her garden, etc.
- *Life is a race.* This person might race through life quickly, doing things rapidly.
- *Life is creation.* This person might focus on creating and transforming things.
- *Life is a merry-go-round.* This person might see life as being enjoyable and fun.

Lakoff and Johnson (1980) also discussed metaphors for life, including the following:

- *Life is a container.* This person might say things such as, "I've had a *full* life. . . . *Get the most out of* life" (p. 51, italics in original).
- *Life is a gamble.* This person might say, "I'll *take my chances. . . .* If you *play your cards right*, you can do it" (p. 51, italics in original).

Others could use different metaphors to describe life:

- *Life is a game of strategy.* In order to be successful, one must think carefully about the next move to make. This person might strategize before making a move and delay acting until certain that the move is the correct one.
- *Life is a game to be won or lost.* One can win the game of life only by overcoming and subduing the opponent. This person might engage in combat when relating with others.
- *Life is an enjoyable game.* One goes from one game to the next with a spirit of fun and anticipation. This person might be playful, joking with others.
- *Life is an adventure.* Each new experience has the potential to be extremely exciting. This person might engage in living with excitement and a sense of adventure.
- *Life is a journey.* We travel from one experience to the next one. This person might move frequently from one thing to another.
- *Life is war.* In order to win, one must overcome and defeat the opponent. This person might want to win at all costs.

What metaphor for living do you hold? Mine used to be that life was a race. I raced everywhere. When I changed my thoughts about the metaphor of a race to define the winner as the one who goes the slowest and enjoys each moment the most, the quality of my life and the quality of my interactions with others increased greatly. According to Faulkner (1991), it is difficult for a person to completely change his or her metaphor from one to another. He suggested working within that metaphor to frame it differently, as I did.

Understanding our own metaphors helps us to understand our students' metaphors. Younger students may not have developed metaphors as completely; however, we can observe the metaphors by which their parents appear to operate. As you think about using inviting language with your students, how might you "tweak" your metaphors for living so that you can truly communicate with caring and respect?

Metaphors for Learning

What does it mean to learn? As you think back over your education, both formal and informal, what is learning to you? Following are some metaphors for teaching and learning:

- Learning is a garden full of lovely flowers. We can pick them to provide beauty in our lives.
- Learning is a race. Whoever gets to the finish line first wins the race.
- Learning is a game of strategy. We can strategize to determine what to learn.
- Learning is a competitive game. We either win or lose.
- Learning is an enjoyable game. We can play it and have a wonderful time.
- Learning is an adventure. We can seek exciting experiences.
- Learning is a journey. We can discover many things each day.
- Learning is war. We must win over the student.
- Learning is a natural process to be enjoyed. We learn every day throughout our lives in many different contexts.

What metaphors about learning do you hold? What is the impact of those metaphors on the students with whom you work? What might be some ways to change the metaphors in order to benefit your students? What metaphors about learning do your students hold? How might you engage them in a discussion of their metaphors and how they affect their learning?

Establishing Rapport

Numerous authors have written about the importance of establishing rapport (Andreas & Faulkner, 1994; Costa & Garmston, 2002; Laborde, 1987; Richardson, 1987). Montgomery (2007) studied the role that mirror neurons play when people communicate. She discovered that when people communicate socially, the mirror neuron system becomes activated. She also found that higher levels of empathy for others are associated with more activity in the mirror neuron system.

The elements of rapport include "posture, gesture, tonality, language, and breathing" (Costa & Garmston, 2007, p. 23). In order to increase our rapport with someone, we can mirror him or her (Laborde, 1987). M. Grinder (personal communication, September 2008) suggested that we can mirror another person's voice as much as 100 percent, another person's face as much as 75 percent, another person's body as much as 50 percent, and another person's gestures while talking 50 to 100 percent. As we mirror other people, we are seeking to be "in sync" with them—we definitely don't want them to think that we are mimicking them—and to help to lead them into more resourceful states and deeper breathing. The elements of rapport are discussed below.

Posture

When two people relate well, their postures tend to be similar (Costa & Garmston, 2007). They might both stand in the same way, they might sit with their legs crossed, or they might lean toward each other. On an unconscious level, somehow, the one whose posture is being mirrored thinks, "The other person is like me." When people feel comfortable, their brain chemistry changes and they are more relaxed. As a result, they are able to put all of their energy into thinking and relating to the other person. In order to facilitate the development of rapport with our students, we can intentionally "mirror" their body posture by sitting or standing in a similar manner. Grinder (2007) suggests positioning one's body at a 90-degree angle from the other person, as opposed to facing the person.

Gestures

Another way to deepen rapport with students is to mirror their gestures to some extent (Costa & Garmston, 2007). We can also reinterpret their gestures; for example, if a student is tapping a pencil, you can move one of your feet in the same rhythm. If a student is tapping his or her foot, you can move your head to the same rhythm.

It is important to truly mirror the other individual's gesture. If a student says, "My mother" and uses a gesture to indicate her on the right side, when you paraphrase and refer to the student's mother, you need to indicate her on your left side, which is the student's right side. By doing so, you reflect the student's gesture as though you are a mirror.

Tone of Voice

We can also deepen rapport with learners by using the same tone of voice that they use (Costa & Garmston, 2007). If they talk in soft voices, we can talk in soft voices. If they talk in louder voices, we can talk in louder voices at first and then soften our voices to lead them into using softer voices. We can also use the same voice inflection that they use. This will help them to feel more comfortable communicating with us.

Language

We can use the same words that our students use in order to deepen rapport with them (Costa & Garmston, 2007). If a student says, "It's terrific," you can repeat back to him or her, "So, it's terrific," in the same tone of voice that the student used. If students habitually use certain words, you can also use them.

Bandler and Grinder (1979) discovered that people use visual, auditory, kinesthetic, olfactory, and gustatory language, with the first three being the most common. These are called representational systems. Yapko (1980) found that people relaxed the most when they heard words corresponding to their primary representational system. When people heard words in their second most preferred representational system, they relaxed slightly less. When they heard words in their third preferred representational system, they relaxed the least. According to Asbell (1983), when counselors matched the representational system words that they used to those used by their clients, the clients rated the counselors as being warmer and less threatening than when counselors used other methods. Hammer (1983) found that

> tracking and matching certain aspects of a speaker's language results in increased perceived empathy. Interviewers who responded by incorporating into their speech words of a type similar to those used by the students were rated higher on empathy compared to interviewers who responded with words of a different type. (p. 177)

In addition to using the words that students use in general, listen for the visual, auditory, and kinesthetic words that they use.

Visual words

Many students describe their experience with visual words:

- "I can *see it clearly* now after having heard the explanation."
- "I want to be able to *visualize* what you want us to do."
- "I want to *have an image* of what the final project will *look like*."
- "I want to be able to *focus* on what I need to do."
- "Right now, what you are telling us is kind of *hazy*."

Repeat back the words that they use:

- "So you want to *be clear* on what you are going to be doing."
- "You want to have a *vivid picture* of what the project will *look like* when you have completed it."

Auditory words

Some students use auditory words to describe their experiences. We have heard people say, "That rings a bell" or "I want to be able to hear what it sounds like." Other examples of auditory language include the following:

- "I'll know it when I *hear* it."
- "I keep *telling myself* that I will be able to do it."
- "Let me *verbalize* it to you to make sure that I understand correctly."
  - "That really sounds *dissonant* to me."
  - "I am doing my best to *tune in to* what you are saying."

Respond with auditory words:
- "So you want to *hear it* in order to know that you know it."
- "So you want to *tell yourself* that you can do it."

Kinesthetic words

Other students use kinesthetic words in expressing themselves

- "I want to *get a grasp* on this assignment."
- "I have a *gut feeling* that this is going to be difficult."
- "I have the weight of the world *on my shoulders.*"
- "I want to *feel* like I know it."
- "This assignment really makes me *feel energetic.*"
- "I'm *feeling a little tense* about doing this project."
- "I really need to *come to grips* with what I am doing."

Respond with kinesthetic words:
- "So you want to have the assignment *in your hands.*"
- "So when you know it, you will have a *certain feeling in your body.*"

Breathing

We have all experienced the feeling of community while singing songs together around the campfire and in other contexts. When people sing together, they are breathing together. Thus, their rapport goes deeper the longer they continue singing.

We can deepen rapport with students by breathing at the same time that they breathe (Costa & Garmston, 2007). As they talk, watch for when they pause to take breaths. Breathe in as they breathe in, and breathe out as they are talking. Watch as their shoulders go up and down, taking breaths with them when their shoulders go up, and breathing out with them as their shoulders go down.

Using Intonation

The language tips in this book can be used in a manner that either draws learners toward us and encourages them or drives learners away from us and discourages them. It all depends on the intonation of our voices.

Grinder (2007) identifies two types of voices that people use, as well as points along the continuum. The friendly type is called an *approachable* voice. He suggests that our voice intonation is only a matter of physiology. When people use an approachable voice, their head goes up and down, and their palms face up. We can see this in the kindergarten teacher who says in a highly approachable voice, "Welcome, boys and girls. We are going to have a wonderful day!" In general, women tend to use more approachable voices than men.

On the other end of the continuum is the *credible* voice (Grinder, 2007). When people talk in this voice, their head remains stationary. At the end of their sentence or phrase, the head goes down. Their palms also face down. We have all been in meetings with people who use approachable voices to make suggestions to the group. They tend to be largely ignored. But when someone says in a highly credible voice, "I think we should do that," with a flat intonation pattern, moving the head down on the last word, everyone says, "We will do that." The people who had previously said the same thing using an approachable voice are left thinking, "I just said that."

Experiment with using both types of voices. You can also combine them and say some words or sentences in an approachable manner and other words or sentences in a credible manner. When we ask for something, it's better to use an approachable voice. Picture a teacher saying, "What are your questions?" in a credible voice, with the voice flat and the head going down at the end of the question. Most students will not respond when asked in this way. Now picture the teacher with palms up, using an approachable voice to ask, "What are your questions?" That teacher will receive far more responses than the first teacher would get.

Breathing

One of our goals in using inviting language with students is to keep them breathing deeply so that oxygen flows to their brains and they are able to learn (Grinder, 2007). We want their abdomens to go in and out while we communicate. When we put them in a relaxed state and make them feel safe, the blood in their bodies is able to flow to the cerebral cortex so that they can think. If they don't feel safe, they begin operating from their "reptilian brain." In this state, the blood flows to the arms and legs so that they can either fight with us or flee from us (the "fight or flight" syndrome).

In order to help students breathe, we must make sure that we are breathing, as well. They tend to model what we do. M. Grinder (personal communication, September 1995) underlined the importance of educators exercising so they can breathe well in the classroom. The more oxygen we take in, the more oxygen our students can take in as they copy us on an unconscious level.

In the early 1990s, I took a sabbatical from teaching and worked for a learning company. My job was to design training for large companies. I was immediately given a huge project to complete within a short time line. I was feeling as though it would be fairly difficult to meet the time line, and I was not breathing as I was sitting at the computer. The level of stress did not exactly help the fluidity of my writing.

As I sat there, fighting back the tears, one of my new colleagues came by to say hello. Seeing my distress, he asked what was wrong. I told him. He said, "Oh, that's easy! MSU!" "MSU?" I responded. He said, "Yeah! Make stuff up!" I burst out laughing. His goal was to make me laugh, which would allow oxygen to flow to the brain, which would allow me to breathe and think, enabling me to write and complete the project on time!

The more we can help students breathe deeply, the more they will be able to learn. A friend of mine who teaches 1st and 2nd grade regularly takes her students outside to jog when she senses that they need to pause and refresh themselves. When they return to the classroom, they are ready to work again. Another friend tells jokes to her students to get them to laugh and breathe. Humor is an extremely effective way of getting a group of students to breathe.

Managing the Classroom

In order to focus on talking invitationally with students, we need to have a well-functioning classroom in which students know what to do (Thompson, 2007). Numerous books have been written to help teachers manage student behavior. *Handbook of Classroom Management* (Evertson & Weinstein, 2006) offers information about setting up a smoothly running classroom. According to *Guiding Children's Behavior* (Flicker & Hoffman, 2006), educators should take a systems approach to working with children by analyzing student misbehavior from many different angles. Teachers can determine the multiple causes of the misbehavior and formulate possible ways of working with the child in order to help the child to be successful. *Discipline with Dignity* (Curwin, Mendler, & Mendler, 2008) suggests that teachers take a proactive approach to working with students in which all students feel valued and respected. *Classroom Management That Works* (Marzano, 2003) provides numerous research-based strategies for managing the classroom.

ENVOY: Your Personal Guide to Classroom Management (Grinder, 2005) offers 31 nonverbal strategies for managing student behavior in the classroom. Grinder talks about four phases of a lesson: getting their attention, teaching, transition to seatwork, and seatwork. He suggests nonverbal methods for teachers to use during each phase. *A Healthy Classroom* (Grinder, 2000) outlines strategies for creating a cohesive class. In addition, *Charisma: The Art of Relationships* (Grinder, 2009) discusses strategies for working with students who are more like cats and those who are more like dogs. We need to approach them differently and treat them differently. Additional resources for classroom management techniques include *Teaching with Love and Logic: Taking Control of the Classroom* (Fay & Funk, 1995) and *The Elusive Obvious: The Science of Non-Verbal Communication* (Grinder, 2007).

What are some of the strategies that you have found to be helpful in managing your classroom so that you can focus on helping students learn?

Aligning with Students' Belief Systems

Has anyone ever made a statement about you that you felt was inaccurate? What were your immediate impulses? When we make statements to students, we need to be sure that they are close enough to the students' reality that the students are able to accept them. Festinger (as cited in Aronson, 1997) developed the concept of "cognitive dissonance." He found that when we make statements that conflict with the reality of others, they tend to go out and prove that we are wrong and they are right.

If we say, "You are really well behaved" to students who don't have that self-concept, they may need to do something to prove that they really aren't well behaved, such as hitting another student. If we say, "You are working hard" when students are loafing or goofing off, they may think we are crazy and feel obliged to goof off even more in order to prove that they are right and we are wrong.

As we use these language tips, it is important to take each student's reality into consideration. By pointing out positive behaviors when we see them, however, little by little, we can help students to see themselves in a positive light. What are some statements that you could make to encourage the learners with whom you work?

2

Arenas in Which the Language Tips Can Be Applied

We use language in nearly every interaction that we have with students and parents. This chapter includes suggestions for applying the language tips in various situations: giving feedback to students; interacting with parents; writing positive notes to students, parents, and colleagues; making positive phone calls; creating positive signs; writing report cards; designing the syllabus; and using technology.

Giving Feedback to Students

We continually give feedback to students about how they are doing. Do students learn better when they feel weak or when they feel strong? Of course, they can learn more effectively when they feel strong. We can use our language to bolster our students and enhance their ability to learn. Before every interaction with a student, ask yourself, "What can I say in order to help this student feel strong?" When you ask students to make corrections on papers, it can be helpful to say "Please do X" as opposed to "Don't do X." If we tell students what we *want* them to do, they will keep that in mind. Likewise, if we tell them what we *do not* want them to do, they will also keep that in mind—and may forget that we said not to do it (Hall, 2004).

Interacting with Parents

We have many interactions with parents, both during parent-teacher conferences and on a daily basis. These language tips can be used in any interaction with parents. Just as our goal is to help our students feel strong, we can make it a goal to help parents feel strong. Parents can accept almost any feedback from a teacher as long as they know that the teacher likes their child. What language could you use to communicate to parents that you really like their child? How could you soften what you say, even if you are delivering information that parents could perceive negatively? How would you speak so that parents will easily accept your message and join you in helping their children succeed?

Writing Positive Notes to Students, Parents, and Colleagues

We all like to hear that we did a good job. When I taught 2nd grade at Wilmot Elementary in Evergreen, Colorado, my principal, Jim Fay, suggested that we write positive notes to students, parents, and colleagues. It was gratifying to see a smile come across a student's face, to receive a call from an elated parent, and to see the appreciation in a colleague's face!

What are some of the positive notes that people have written to you, thanking you for doing something and pointing out something positive about yourself? I have a file in which I save the positive notes that people have taken the time to write to me over a lifetime. We can cherish those notes forever!

What could you write to students to point out positive characteristics that you have noticed? Consider the following statements:

- "You are really working hard today!"
- "Thank you for coming in from recess on time!"
- "The person on lunchroom duty today gave you a compliment. She said that you always help clean the table!" (People love to hear secondhand compliments.)

You can write notes like the following to parents:

- "John worked hard today and completed his assignments."
- "Sally played cooperatively on the playground today."
- "Bill got 100% on his test today."
- "Tom helped a friend who was feeling low."

You can also write positive notes to colleagues. It only takes a minute of your time and helps to build powerful relationships! Some examples include the following:

- "Thank you for helping with recess duty today."
- "You were so kind to come to my aid in the lunchroom today!"
- "How nice of you to take my place on bus duty today when I needed to meet with a parent! How about going for coffee Friday afternoon? It's on me!"

Making Positive Phone Calls

Another tip for showing students that we care and building a relationship with them is to make positive phone calls to parents. Based on a recommendation from Jim Fay early in my teaching career, I made it a point to call all parents during the first week or two of each school year to say something positive about their child. "Hi, this is Jenny Edwards, _____'s teacher. I just wanted to let you know that it is a pleasure having _____ in my class. I've noticed that _____ really enjoys doing artwork (or whatever)." I never ceased to be amazed at the excitement of students when they came to school the next day and said, "You called my mom last night and told her you were glad that I was in your classroom!"

When you call parents during the first several weeks of school, you can't be expected to give a full report on the student's progress. Thus, the calls only last a few minutes. You are going beyond the call of duty in the parents' eyes, and they appreciate the opportunity to get to know you a little bit and know that you like their child. I also made it a point to call each parent at least once during each school quarter to touch base. As a classroom teacher, I am a salesperson—representing both myself and what I am teaching. I want my students' parents to be telling them positive things about me so that they will be open and eager to learn. Wlodkowski and Jaynes (1990) emphasized the importance of a strong teacher-parent connection for motivating students to learn.

When I was invited to interview for a job at the middle school level, the assistant principal asked me how I handled problems with parents. I said that I didn't have any. After just about falling out of his chair, he asked how I managed that. I said that I called parents at the beginning of the year to establish rapport with them. Then I continued calling them as needed throughout the year, at least once a quarter. He said that it would be difficult for me to do at the middle school level, because I would be working with more than 150 students. I said that it was even more important for me to call all of the parents. I would love to say that the middle school students were as thrilled as the elementary students that I was in frequent contact with their parents! Still, the time that I spent on the phone talking with parents paid enormous dividends.

Creating Positive Signs

We immediately know when we enter a building whether it has an invitational climate or a climate in which we do not feel welcome. You can create positive signs for your classroom and school. At the entrance to schools, we usually see signs directing people to go to the office to check in. Which sign makes you feel more welcome?

- "You MUST report to the office."
or
- "Please come to the office so that we can welcome you."

I recently visited a high school library. The sign on the door read:

- "If you bring drinks or food into the library, you will IMMEDI-ATELY be sent to the office."
versus
- "Please dispose of food and drink before entering the library so that we can keep it neat and clean."

How might you weave invitational language into the signs that you create?

Writing Report Cards

Think about when you were in school. What was your experience when you read on your report card, "_____ doesn't do her work"? The brain tends to think that this proclamation refers to the past, present, and future, for all time. So why try?

How does the following sentence change your experience? "_____ does _____, _____, _____, and _____ well. She might bene-fit from working even harder in the area of _____." The little word "even" implies that the student is already doing something well and could be doing it even better. People are always able to improve what they are doing. Even the most accomplished artist can do bet-ter and, in fact, is continually seeking to do better. The word "even" implies that the person is building on strengths, not on deficits.

When I taught 2nd grade, Jim Fay told me everything that I was doing well when I went in for my teacher evaluation. I knew the areas of my teaching that I wanted to improve. He only focused on the things that I did well, though. I kept waiting to hear the negatives, and they never came. As a result of that experience, I liked him so much that I wanted to be the best teacher I could be.

What happens when people tell us things that we do well? What happens when we point out things that students do well?

Designing the Syllabus

As you write your course syllabus, keep the language tips in mind. You want the syllabus to be inviting to students, and you want them to feel uplifted as they read it. Instead of making a statement such as "You must do X," you might say, "Please do X" or "You may find the following resources to be helpful."

Using Technology

You can use the language tips in this book when you use technology with students. Warlick (2007) has provided information for educators who are interested in using technology in the classroom. His book contains step-by-step instructions for getting started, as well as ideas for assignments that teachers can use for blogs, wikis, podcasting, online message boards, and other types of technology. Clyde and Delohery (2005) have also provided a helpful book on using technology to streamline what we are already doing. This section includes possible applications for the language tips in blogs, bulletin boards, chat rooms, e-mails, multiuser virtual environments, podcasting, PowerPoint presentations, text messages, and wikis.

Blogs

You can set up blogs to communicate with students and others on the Internet. Warlick's (2007) book contains step-by-step instructions for setting up blogs using Blogger (www.blogger.com). You can invite your students to publish their writing and observations on the blog. According to Warlick, educators and their students can write about what is happening in the world, the rationale behind what they are doing in the classroom, classroom events, and many other areas. You can weave the language tips into all of these areas.

A Google search on blogs for teachers brought up some helpful Web sites. At TeacherWeb (www.teacherweb.com), teachers can customize blogs for their classrooms. The portal 21Classes (www.21classes.com) provide a location for student blogs as well. At Blogs for Teachers (http://blogsforteachers.info) and Gaggle.Net (www.gaggle.net), educators can create blogs for their students. Finally, at Teacher Lingo (http://teacherlingo.com), educators at all levels can share ideas with each other via blogs.

Bulletin Boards

According to Warlick (2007), educators can set up bulletin boards at Nicenet (http://nicenet.org) so that students can engage in discussions. You can write messages to individual students in response to their postings on bulletin boards that all will see. You can also write messages on bulletin boards to students in general. You can consciously choose the goal that you want to achieve through the language you use. For example, at the beginning of a year or a term, students might introduce themselves on a bulletin board. You can respond to each individual student's posting with words of encouragement. You can also paraphrase what each student said and pose questions for further thought. You can network students together (e.g., "_____ also mentioned that") and share commonalities (e.g., "I also have that interest").

Chat Rooms

You can use the material in this book in Internet chat rooms, as well. You can coach students, paraphrasing what they are saying and asking questions. You can also watch for the visual, auditory, and kinesthetic words that they are using and use similar words in your responses to them (Edwards, Ellison, Mitchell, & Thiru, 2003). You can use all of the language tips just as if you were talking in person.

E-mails

You can send e-mails to members of your classes—group e-mails as well as individual e-mails. This provides you with even more time to consciously formulate a response to students. For example, when a student writes about a problem in an e-mail, you can ask yourself, "What can I say that will encourage and empower this student?" You might paraphrase what the student said: "So you are feeling upset because of the situation, and what you want is to be successful, and you are looking for ways to do that." (This is from the "problem resolving conversation" that Costa and Garmston [2002] discuss.) Then, you might ask the student a question such as, "In other past situations in which you have been successful, what were some of the strategies that you used to succeed?" Whatever you write, you can consciously choose your goal—to help students feel strong, to let students know that you understand what they are saying, to stimulate the students' creativity, to encourage students to think, to help students to visualize being successful, and so on.

Multiuser Virtual Environments

You can also use the language tips in Multiuser Virtual Environments (MUVEs), Internet-based three-dimensional environments in which educators and others around the world use avatars, online three-dimensional characters, to interact with one another in environments that are similar to the real world. Avatars can take the shape of the individual, or they can be an animal or other creature. Second Life (www.secondlife.com), by Linden Labs, is a popular MUVE that enables educators to talk online with people around the world through avatars. Universities and businesses are increasingly developing a presence in Second Life. Some other MUVEs include There (www.there.com) and Active Worlds (www.activeworlds.com).

You can also use the language tips in Massively Multiplayer Online Role-Playing Games (MMORPGs) to accomplish goals in a game format. MMORPGs are fantasy environments in which people interact in a gaming context. As in MUVEs, players use avatars to work together in teams to accomplish quests, interact socially, and seek to improve their skills. World of Warcraft (www. WorldofWarcraft.com), Dungeons and Dragons (www.wizards.com/ dnd), and EverQuest (everquest.station.sony.com) are three of the many MMORPGs that are available.

Podcasting

What are the purposes of the podcast? Do we want to encourage our students, provide them with information, stimulate their thinking, inspire them, or share our ideas? Warlick (2007) suggests putting lectures on a podcast and having students listen to them prior to attending class. Then, you can use class time to discuss what students have already heard.

In a podcast, you could interview individual students to introduce them to the other students. What questions could you ask to bring out the best in those students and tap their individual interests in order to network them with other students?

You can also make daily announcements to the students in your classes using podcasting. Once again, you can determine the purposes for creating each of the messages for them. How would you like the students to feel as a result of your message? What would you like to inspire them to do? Would you like for them to feel creative? Empowered? Enthusiastic? Curious? You can convey those emotions through the stories you tell, as well as through your own demeanor in the podcasts.

Warlick (2007) suggests accessing the Education Podcast Network (http://epnweb.org) to see the variety of podcasts that educators have created. Podcasts can be recorded with a microphone that connects to the computer. Warlick also recommends Audacity (http://audacity.sourceforge.net), which provides a free program for editing podcasts. The Partners in Rhyme Web site (www. partnersinrhyme.com) contains royalty-free sound effects and music. Podcasts can be uploaded for broadcasting into PodOmatic (www.podomatic.com).

PowerPoint Presentations

You can weave the language tips into your PowerPoint presentations as well. In addition to presenting the information that you want to communicate to the students, you can invite them to engage in various activities to process the information. You might write, "Please find a partner at another table and have a two-minute standing conversation about the information." You could also add, "As you talk, please brainstorm possible answers to the following questions."

Text Messages

You might want to send text messages to your students. You can use the language tips in this book to communicate with them. You can even develop your own abbreviations for the various positive things that you might tell them through text messages.

Wikis

Wikis, or collaborative Web sites, can be set up at Wikispaces (www.wikispaces.com). In wikis, students can edit each others' work. Warlick (2007) provides numerous suggestions for using wikis with students, such as inviting teams of students to work together on projects, creating dictionary pages for the class, asking students to add to each others' stories, and collaborating on developing documents.

Numerous resources are available on the Internet for those who might be new to using wikis. A Google search on "wikis for teachers" brought up a number of Web sites. The TeachersFirst.com Wiki Walk-Through (www.teachersfirst.com/content/wiki) provides basic information about using wikis in the classroom, including topics such as a definition of wikis, ideas for using them in teaching, and wiki tools to get started. At Wikis in Education (wikisineducation. wetpaint.com), educators at all levels can network, ask questions, and share ideas about using wikis in their classrooms.

3

Strategies for Using the Language Tips with Various Types of Students

The language tips in this book can be used with students of all ages. Of course, you are the expert on the needs of the students with whom you work. This chapter provides some suggestions for implementing the tips with special needs students, diverse populations, various ages of students, and students in the online environment.

Special Needs Students

You will know best how to use the language tips most effectively with your special needs students. You may need to simplify the language that you use, depending on the needs of the student.

James (2008) suggests that children with special needs benefit from simple instructions given in a step-by-step format. For younger children, she recommends beginning with one-step directions, such as "Please pick up the pencil." When the child can follow one-step instructions, you can add a second step, such as "Please pick up the pencil and draw a straight line." Then you can give three instructions at a time. She also suggests that for elementary students, we should underline or highlight the verbs in our written instructions, such as "<u>Subtract</u> the two numbers" or "<u>Write</u> T for 'true' or F for 'false.'" For middle school and high school special needs students, James suggests standing close to students when explaining what they need to do. She also recommends writing the instructions for students so that they can refer to them.

Bryant, Smith, and Bryant (2008) discuss the importance of teachers building relationships with special needs students, introducing the lesson, providing information, and allowing the students to practice what they learn. They also suggest that teachers should be clear with students about rules and the consequences for not obeying them, send messages that are clear, and give concise instructions to students. One of my colleagues has a son with special needs who is extremely sensitive to voice tone. She tells me that she has to be careful to use a pleasant voice around him, even when talking with her other children. If she doesn't, he can easily become upset.

Diverse Populations of Students

Ladson-Billings (1994) cites a study in which the most effective teachers of Native American students "altered their speech patterns, communication styles, and participation structures to resemble more closely those of the students' own culture" (p. 16). We can use rapport skills for creating culturally appropriate learning environments so that all students in our classes feel welcome and included. We can use their language, mirror their body posture and gestures, use the tone of voice and words that they use, and breathe when they breathe (Costa & Garmston, 2007).

According to Davis (2007), building community in a classroom is essential. She talks about how relaxed we feel when we are with our family and friends, part of the community. "Community is where you feel accepted and loved. It is where you feel your voice counts" (p. 67). She recounts a story of a 5th grade teacher who did not send any students to the office for misbehaving. The teacher attributed it to focusing on building community during the first two weeks of school.

Holcomb-McCoy (2000) discusses the importance of realizing how students' culture influences their "way of thinking, belief systems, definitions-of-self, decision making, verbal and non-verbal behavior, and time orientation" (p. 8). In addition, she believes that it is important to adjust our nonverbal communication, such as how close we stand to students, to align with their culture. According to Davis (2007), "when we do not understand the communication cues of our diverse learners, we may be telling them (unintentionally) that we do not care enough about them to learn about them" (p. 15).

Ladson-Billings (1994) suggests that culturally relevant teachers emphasize the importance of each individual student and are "consciously working to develop commonalities with all students" (p. 66). This is particularly important given the rate at which many families move from school to school. Ream and Stanton-Salazar (2007) encourage teachers to make the effort to get to know new students, even though they may not be there for a long time. Margaret Rossi, a teacher in Ladson-Billings's study of teachers who are effective with African American students, invites students to fill out a questionnaire in which she asks them about their interests, what they do in their spare time, their favorite subjects in school, and other likes and dislikes. Then she develops her year's program around their interests and strengths. She talks with them during the year and develops commonalities with them. Rossi also puts birthday cards on students' desks on their birthdays to acknowledge their special day. According to Ladson-Billings, "Such personal acknowledgments support the students' sense of self—they are seen as 'real people' by their teacher" (p. 67).

Baskin (2002) discusses the importance of creating a curriculum that addresses the range of student diversity. According to Baskin, "all students need to see themselves represented in the physical landscape of the school and classroom" (p. 3). In addition to having "books, posters, art, etc." (p. 3), teachers need to truly understand the students' cultures. Ginsberg and Wlodkowski (2000) talk about the importance of creating inclusive environments in which all students feel welcome. They suggest "four conditions of the motivational framework":

1. Establishing inclusion

2. Developing a positive attitude

3. Enhancing meaning

4. Engendering competence (p. 45)

In order to create inclusive classrooms in which all students feel accepted, it is also important to include multiple cultures in discussions. Numerous authors have discussed the importance of telling stories and including information and literature about the many contributions of people representing diverse cultures (e.g., Baskin, 2002; Ginsberg, 2004; Ginsberg & Wlodkowski, 2000; Ladson-Billings, 1994; Wlodkowski & Ginsberg, 1995). In addition, Rong and Brown (2007) recommend encouraging American-born black students to get to know black immigrants. All students would greatly benefit from getting to know students from other backgrounds, according to Paik (2007).

Other authors (e.g., Lee, 2007; Maldonado Torres, 2008; Zhou, 2007) have discussed the importance of teachers realizing that each broad ethnic group includes people from many different countries with diverse values and traditions. Lee talks about the vast differences between students from Japan and Asian students from less affluent countries, such as Hmong students. Maldonado Torres found differences in learning styles between Latino students from different Spanish-speaking countries. Thus, we need to be cautious about making generalizations about all students from a particular broad ethnic group and instead get to know each individual student.

Davis (2007) emphasizes the importance of educators understanding the style of communication that students use. She discusses the "call-and-response patterns found in Black music" (p. 15) and recommends incorporating these patterns into classroom lessons. Delpit (1988) suggests that African American children are accustomed to receiving direct commands from their parents, such as "Sit down." When white teachers use indirect commands, such as "Would you like to sit down?," African American students may believe that they have a choice of what to do and subsequently choose not to sit down. This results in the perception that the student is disobeying, when in reality, the student was making what he or she believed was a valid choice.

According to Davis (2007), Native American students need a long period of wait time (Rowe, 1986) before responding to questions because they learn to "think deliberately and respond more slowly after considering all options" (Davis, 2007, p. 15). She also suggests that cooperative learning is more consistent with their culture than competition.

According to Delgado-Gaitan (2007), it is essential that Latino students, particularly Latina girls, receive messages about going to college and succeeding. Thompson (2007) echoes the thought for African American students. Davis (2007) and Waxman, Padrón, and García (2007) suggest using cooperative learning with Latino students more than competitive formats, as they are taught to value cooperating.

Above all, we must truly believe that all of our students are capable of learning, and we must communicate those high expectations to them (Paik, 2007). We can help them to see themselves pursuing degrees in higher education and continuing to learn throughout their lives. We can talk with them about the benefits of learning in terms of increased salary, better quality of life, and so on, and we can ensure that they learn both the skills and the mind-set that will assist them in moving forward (Thompson, 2007).

Various Ages of Students

The language tips can be used with students at preschool, primary, intermediate, middle school, high school, undergraduate, master's, and doctoral levels. They can be used with children as well as with adults. Younger students may need to have simpler statements and questions than older students; however, the same guidelines apply to all levels. Chapter 5 offers sample statements at various age levels of students in various contexts.

Students in the Online Environment

The language tips can be used just as easily in the online environment as in person. Aune (2002) investigated students who were conducting action research in an online environment at the master's level. She found that the students' relationships with the instructor were critical to the students' progress and attitude. The students valued feeling supported, having their ideas respected, and feeling cared about. Aune suggests that the way that faculty members worded their responses to students affected the students' perceptions of support and relationship. Since faculty teaching in distributed schools aren't able to communicate caring nonverbally to their

---

The following books contain helpful information about creating culturally responsive classrooms:

- *How to Teach Students Who Don't Look Like You: Culturally Relevant Teaching Strategies,* Bonnie M. Davis, 2007
- *Building Culturally Responsive Classrooms: A Guide for K–6 Teachers,* Concha Delgado-Gaitan, 2006
- *Culturally Responsive Teaching: Theory, Research, and Practice,* Geneva Gay, 2000
- *The Dreamkeepers: Successful Teachers of African American Children,* Gloria Ladson-Billings, 1994
- *Diversity and Motivation: Culturally Responsive Teaching,* Raymond Wlodkowski and Margery Ginsberg, 1995

students, they need to pay particular attention to the words they use in order to encourage students who are often working in isolation. By stating things positively rather than negatively, they can help students to feel good about their work. Instead of saying, "This paper needs work," and "The paper is okay, but . . . ," they might say, "Here are some ways to make the paper *even* better."

4

Possible Purposes for Using the Language Tips

The 100 language tips in this book can be used for many purposes, including building relationships with students, teaching, helping students plan for the future, responding to student objections, encouraging students, influencing students, and resolving conflicts.

Building Relationships with Students

Howard and Johnson (2000) asked both students and teachers what made the difference between students with difficult lives who succeeded and those who didn't succeed. Both teachers and students discussed the importance of teachers providing relationships of support and caring. Students also talked about the importance of teachers teaching effectively so that students could learn the skills they needed to succeed.

Peggy Valentine, a teacher in Ladson-Billings's (1994) study, said, "In order to help [the students] develop some motivation, I capitalize on their strong feelings for me" (p. 44). According to Ladson-Billings, "good teaching starts with building good relationships" (p. 125). Wlodkowski (1986) suggests that when learners have a positive attitude toward the instructor, they will be more motivated to learn.

Teaching

As we teach, we can use language mindfully to help students learn even more quickly. According to Forsyth and colleagues (1998), "teacher talk that is clear and explicit empowers learners, especially struggling readers and writers" (p. 9). When they studied how teachers interacted with their students, they found that expert teachers clearly explained to students what they wanted them to do. They created specific learning goals and communicated them clearly to students. They provided feedback to students, and they helped students to reflect on what they did. They concluded that "clear instruction does not occur by happenstance but results from a set of instructional actions that teachers use consciously to promote learning" (p. 15).

Rowe (1998) suggested that teachers are more likely to focus more on arranging the physical layout of the classroom than on what they say to encourage learning in their students. She added that teachers generally tend not to be aware of their talk and how it impacts students and their learning. In order to focus on the language that she used with students, she devised questions that she regularly asked herself: "How can I learn to talk differently with students? What other changes in the classroom environment are necessary to support changes in my talk and that of my students?" (p. 106). What might be some questions that you could be asking yourself on a daily basis as you are interacting with students whom you teach?

Planning for the Future

We all know from personal experience the importance of planning—particularly planning for the long term. Students who can look into the future and see themselves next week, next month, next year, 5 years in the future, 10 years in the future, and more tend to be more successful in planning and succeeding than students who can only see tomorrow or perhaps the next day.

Numerous studies have been done on how students view time, or *time orientation*. Students who focus on the future have a *future time orientation*. According to Stouthard and Peetsma (1999), when students are focused on the future, they are more motivated and will work harder to accomplish their goals. De Volder and Lens (1982) found that students who had high grade point averages and effective study habits believed that distant future goals were important. They also believed that they should study hard to achieve those goals more than students who had low grade point averages and tended not to study as much. In another study, Brown and Jones (2004) found that "consistent with the results of prior investigations, African American students with high levels of future orientation tended to also have higher grades" (p. 266). They added that "a strong future orientation [is] an important resilience factor with respect to academic achievement. This study joins a number of others that indicate that a strong future orientation is associated not only with higher academic motivation but performance as well" (p. 267).

Responding to Student Objections

Have you ever temporarily perceived that you couldn't do something, or that a task was too difficult for you? You may have said, "I can't do that," "I don't want to do that," "I don't have time to do that," or you may have said that you would do it and then didn't. You may have even made excuses about why you couldn't do it to preserve your self-esteem.

When you had those perceptions, what were some of the strategies that you used to overcome them? Did someone else say something to you to change your perceptions? Did you talk to yourself and convince yourself that you could do the task? Did you just forge ahead, buckle down, and do the task? Did you walk away and not even try?

From time to time, students may have objections to what we ask of them. They might say that they can't do what we would like them to do. They might say that they don't want to do a task. They may have positive intentions, perhaps wanting to preserve their self-esteem, use their time doing other things, or maintain dignity. They may perceive, on an unconscious level, that they will be more able to maintain their dignity by not doing what we are asking them to do than by doing it and risking not doing it well or failing. The language tips provide strategies for responding to students' objections and finding ways to overcome them.

Encouraging Students

Have you ever felt like you just wanted someone to encourage you? You may have felt stuck, not knowing where to turn for help. You may have just wanted someone to notice you, affirm you, and tell you that you were doing a good job. All of us have felt that way at some time in our lives. Our students benefit from receiving encouraging words, too! As we encourage learners, they bond with us and want to achieve even more in order to please us!

Golden and colleagues (2005) studied students who had dropped out of high school and completed their General Educational Development (GED) high school equivalency diploma. The purpose of the study was to explore the students' reasons for dropping out of school. The researchers found that, in addition to organizational "red tape" the students had experienced, they reported that they had longed for teachers to care about them and to express that caring. They were pleased that at the college level, teachers were on a more equal basis with students and were more accessible to them.

Golden and colleagues report that the students "remembered comments from teachers that were received as subtly denigrating. . . . Often students could point to a single comment from a teacher that had made a difference in their lives" (2005, p. 313). The authors suggest that teachers should pay attention to students' home lives and notice their students enough to talk with them and show that they care: "Our participants were crying out for a kind word from a teacher" (p. 315).

In a study of middle school students, Cline (1995) found that students want two things from their teachers.

> First, students want teachers who care for them. Second, students want teachers who think of them as individuals. . . . [They want teachers to] care in terms of "I care enough for you to encourage you, be sensitive to you, show pleasure with you and your friends, help you, be joyful, create trust, and just appreciate you." (pp. 82–83)

Influencing Students

We are in an important position to influence students for good. Stories abound about teachers who changed the course of students' lives. A major tool that we have in influencing students is the language we use. We can skillfully use language to affect students' lives, with repercussions that last many years into the future.

Resolving Conflicts

The language tips can be used for resolving conflicts between students. We can use them ourselves, and we can teach them to students to enable them to resolve their own conflicts and the conflicts of their peers. Schrumpf and colleagues (1997) suggest that peer mediators should listen carefully to what both parties are saying, paraphrase their concerns, and ask open-ended questions. They believe that educators have the responsibility of creating safe places for students and helping them learn responsible behavior. They also discuss reframing and wondering as possible techniques for mediators to use. They suggest that conflicts result from "limited resources," "unmet basic needs," and "different values" (p. 125).

Schrumpf and colleagues (1997) identify the following steps in the peer mediation process:

Step 1: Agree to mediate

Step 2: Gather points of view

Step 3: Focus on interests

Step 4: Create win-win options

Step 5: Evaluate the options

Step 6: Create agreement (p. 145)

In Step 1, in which the participants consent to go through mediation, peer mediators provide a definition of mediation. They inform the participants that the mediators will remain neutral, that what is said needs to be kept confidential, that the participants will both have turns at sharing and listening, and that everyone will need to cooperate. The mediators invite participants to agree to abide by the rules.

In Step 2, the mediators ask both parties to explain what happened. Mediators paraphrase what the participants say and invite both participants to add to what has been said and share their feelings about the situation.

In Step 3, mediators attempt to surface underlying interests. They ask the participants what they want and why. They listen, paraphrase, and ask each participant to step into the shoes of the other participant. They may also ask about the results if the two people are not able to resolve the situation. They summarize each participant's interests and attempt to find common ground.

In Step 4, mediators invite participants to brainstorm win-win possibilities. They explain the rules of brainstorming (i.e., say whatever comes to mind, avoid judging, generate numerous options, come up with creative ideas) and write down the participants' ideas.

In Step 5, mediators ask participants to evaluate the various ideas that they brainstormed. They ask if the option is fair, if it can be done, and the extent to which it might work.

In Step 6, mediators ask the participants to develop a specific plan. They write down the plan and ask both participants to summarize what they have agreed to do. Then, they end the mediation.

Gilhooley and Scheuch (2000) suggest that mediators use paraphrases such as, "'So you're feeling _____ because _____'" (p. 29). They emphasize that when people have different points of view, conflict may result. Teolis (2002) created conflict-resolution exercises for helping students develop positive identities, feel like they belong, realize what they value, identify their feelings, express empathy, and communicate effectively. Language tips for all of these are included in this book.

5

100 Tips for Talking Effectively with Your Students

This chapter contains 100 tips for talking with students. Possible uses for the tips are included on pages 153–157 and are summarized after each tip. Feel free to adapt the tips to fit your situation and style. Experiment with them and notice your students' responses.

1. Acknowledging Learners' Current Experience

Have you ever felt reluctant about a new learning situation, like a weekend workshop? Perhaps you had things you would rather do than attend the class. Maybe you were preoccupied by things going on in your family. We've all been there. What if the instructor verbally acknowledged that you were choosing to give up a weekend in order to continue growing professionally? You would relax, knowing that the instructor understood!

It is important to acknowledge your students' current experience. You might say, "It may have been a little bit difficult to leave home this morning, as you had things on your mind. Thank you so much for coming. I'd like to invite you to set those things aside and focus entirely on these experiences so that you can benefit from our time together."

After summer vacation, you might say, "I am sure that you had a wonderful summer vacation and that you were doing many fun and exciting things with your families and friends. The weather was lovely, and I understand that you may be missing it a little bit. We will be outside doing projects so that we can continue enjoying the good weather. We will also be doing a lot of physical activities outside, and you will continue to be with your friends. Thank you for being here."

Potential Functions for This Tip: Building Relationships, Teaching, Planning for the Future, Responding to Objections, Encouraging Students, Resolving Conflicts

2. Adverbs

What is it about the ability of words that end in *-ly* to convey positive things even more powerfully? Use words that end in *-ly* to increase the intensity of your students' experience and help students to feel excited about what you are discussing. It's amazing how using these words will not only encourage students but make you feel good as well!

We can use adverbs such as the following:

- absolutely
- beautifully
- completely
- confidently
- continually
- delightfully
- easily
- elegantly
- enthusiastically
- excitedly
- friendly
- fully
- gladly

- gratefully
- happily
- heartily
- hopefully
- intensely
- internally
- joyfully
- lovely
- possibly
- powerfully
- probably
- quickly
- rapidly
- readily
- skillfully
- spontaneously
- steadily
- strategically
- successfully
- totally
- warmly
- wonderfully

Here are some examples of such adverbs in practice:

- "You will be surprised and delighted at just how *quickly* you are learning the material."
- "As you are working *steadily,* you may notice just how *delightfully* you are progressing."
- "As you are *continually* progressing toward your goal of ____, you may notice just how *instinctively* you are applying your new learnings and understandings."
- "In the process of completing your assignments, you may be pleased with just how *spontaneously* you are doing the work."

- "As you complete this class, you may be noticing just how *rapidly* you have internalized your insights and understandings in order to bring about lasting changes in your life and in the lives of others."
- "I'm sure you are pleased as you realize how *steadily* you have been progressing toward your goals."
- "In what ways might you *skillfully* and *enthusiastically* apply all of the exciting things that you are learning?"
- "This is *absolutely* the hardest-working group of learners that I have seen in my 20-year career!"
- "As you *fully* involve yourself in the process of learning, you may notice just how *quickly* and *easily* you are grasping these concepts!"

Potential Functions for This Tip: Building Relationships, Teaching, Planning for the Future, Responding to Objections, Encouraging Students, Influencing Students, Resolving Conflicts

3. "After . . ."

You can visualize success for students and help them to do the same. Sometimes, students have difficulty visualizing themselves succeeding. Through your language, invite students to go into the future and experience what it is like to have already succeeded in what they are doing.

A woman on a plane once taught me Sudoku, saying, "After you get really good at it, you will do puzzles like these" (she showed me one that looked really complicated). She was helping me to visualize the future, seeing myself having already mastered Sudoku puzzles and working on ones that were even more difficult. When you say "after," you are presupposing that the student will definitely be doing the things that come after it.

- "*After* you have learned this, what else might you enjoy learning?"

- "*After* you have done everything that you identified as necessary to achieve your goals, how will you feel about having been successful?"
- "*After* you have achieved your dreams and even more than you ever thought possible, what will your life be like?"
- "*After* you have put away your materials, you will have a clean desk."
- "*After* you have studied for your test, you will be able to make a good grade."
- "*After* you have written your paper, you will feel really good about what you have accomplished."
- "*After* you have overcome your habit of procrastinating, you will be able to do anything that you want to do in your life!"

Potential Functions for This Tip: Teaching, Planning for the Future, Responding to Objections, Encouraging Students, Influencing Students, Resolving Conflicts

4. "And" or "Yet"—No "Buts"

How do you feel when you hear the word "but"? You probably brace yourself for what might be coming. The other shoe is about to drop. We tend to negate everything that a person says before they say "but"; the word cancels what came before (Hall, 2004).

- "You did a really nice job, but . . ."
- "I like that, but . . ."
- "You could go out to recess, but . . ."

The next time you are tempted to use the word "but," replace it with "and." If "and" doesn't fit, use "yet."

- "You did a really nice job, *and* . . ."
- "I like that, *and* . . ."
- "You could go out to recess, *and* . . ."

On the other hand, you can also use the word "but" to your advantage.

- "I don't know how to do this."
- ○ "*But* you will learn!"
- "I am not succeeding."
- ○ "*But* you will get it soon!"
- "I can't do this."
- ○ "*But* you did it the last time!"

Potential Functions for This Tip: Building Relationships, Teaching, Planning for the Future, Responding to Objections, Encouraging Students, Influencing Students, Resolving Conflicts

5. "As . . ."

As you read this book, you may find that you automatically think of students with whom you will use the various ideas and concepts. As you plan for tomorrow, you may notice those students applying all that they learn and even more.

When you begin sentences with "as," you link the first clause with the second clause. This also enables your listener to link the information in both clauses.

- "*As* you do this assignment, you may notice that you are learning even more."
- "*As* you complete your work today, you may become aware of your growing skills and capabilities."
- "*As* you read this assignment, you may notice just how quickly you are comprehending all that you read."
- "*As* you move toward completing your degree, you may feel absolutely pleased with the many ways that you are progressing."

Potential Functions for This Tip: Teaching, Planning for the Future, Responding to Objections, Encouraging Students, Influencing Students, Resolving Conflicts

6. "At This Time . . ."

Have you ever had different perceptions about the same situation at different times? We all do, depending on what we think about the situation at any given time.

You can help students realize that they will have varying views about their abilities and situations at different times. Yesterday, they might have perceived that they couldn't do something. Today is a new day, and tomorrow is another new day. Do you recall ever thinking that you couldn't do something that was important to you that you subsequently learned to do? Looking back now, the thought that you ever believed that you couldn't do it seems fairly ridiculous!

Our perceptions about various events in our lives can also change from day to day. Use words about time combined with words such as "perception," "seems," and so on to help students realize that their perceptions are not set in stone.

- "So *at that time*, you had *perceived* that task to be difficult."
- "So *right now*, you *feel* that you don't yet know what to do."
- "*At that time*, you *believed* that you couldn't do it."
- "So *at this point in time*, it *seems* like you don't yet have the ability to perform the task."

Potential Functions for This Tip: Planning for the Future, Responding to Objections, Encouraging Students, Influencing Students, Resolving Conflicts

7. "Because" and "Since"

We all want to reap the benefits of what we are doing, don't we? Communicate to students that they are reaping the benefits of the work they are doing by using phrases such as "because" and "since."

- "*Because* you worked hard, you succeeded."
- "*Since* you realized the importance of learning these things, you are progressing rapidly in your studies."
- "*Because* you are attending this seminar, you will gain valuable strategies to use to accelerate your success."

- "*Since* you worked collaboratively in your group, you completed the project in only three days."
- "*Because* you made the decision to learn and grow in many different ways, you have already brought that about in your life."
- "*Since* you focused on completing this assignment, you feel really good about it."

Potential Functions for This Tip: Teaching, Planning for the Future, Responding to Objections, Encouraging Students, Influencing Students, Resolving Conflicts

8. Becoming Someone Else

Who are some of your heroes? Who are the people who can do the things that you would like to learn to do or do even better? When we want to do something better, we can step in and become someone else. Several years ago, I wanted to learn how to get away from work when I was on vacation. A friend suggested that I think of someone who was able to do that with ease. I identified my role model, worked to be like that person, and had a wonderful holiday!

Students have many heroes in their lives, both in person and in the media. When students hesitate to believe that they can actually do something, or when they don't quite yet have the confidence to move forward into completing a task or assignment, ask them about their heroes: "Who might be able to do this quickly and really enjoy doing it?"

This technique helps students move from having no idea what to do, to thinking about how a powerful person in their lives might go about doing something, to actually becoming the person who can do it.

- "What might _____ do in this situation?"
- "What are your thoughts as to how _____ might go about completing this assignment?"
- "What steps might _____ follow in the process of doing this?"

- "If you were _____, what might be some of your thoughts about how to do this?"
- "Step in and become _____. Notice what you are doing as you complete this project."

Potential Functions for This Tip: Planning for the Future, Responding to Objections, Encouraging Students, Influencing Students, Resolving Conflicts

9. "Before Friday" Instead of "By Friday"

What does it mean when someone asks you to do something "by Friday"? Most people visualize themselves completing the task on Thursday evening, stressed out because they are doing it at the last minute. What do you visualize when someone says, "Please do this before Friday"? This change in wording allows the listener to focus on the time before Friday, perhaps even the entire week that precedes Friday.

Frequently, we ask students to have something completed "by Friday." Instead, use the term "before Friday" to help students envision the whole process of completing the assignment, and they will be more likely to focus on the time during the prior week, according to C. Hall (personal communication, May 2006).

- "Please complete your project *before* spring break."
- "Papers will be due *before* the end of the day on Wednesday."
- "Please turn in your work *before* the end of class tomorrow."
- "Papers are due *before* 3 p.m. today."

Potential Functions for This Tip: Teaching, Planning for the Future, Influencing Students, Resolving Conflicts

10. "By Doing X . . ."

By teaching, we affect the future. By focusing on encouraging students, we help them to be powerful learners who will encourage others. By encouraging others, your students will powerfully influence the world! By beginning a sentence with "By doing X," we imply that the student is definitely going to be reaping certain benefits as a result of doing something.

- *"By studying* the material every night after class, you will almost guarantee that you will do well on the final exam."
- *"By participating* in class, you will build relationships with your colleagues that can last a lifetime."
- *"By coming* to class every day and taking notes, you will ensure that you do well in the class."
- *"By walking* quietly down the hall between classes, you enable students in other classes to continue studying."
- *"By being willing* to take risks and do new things, you will grow more than you ever dreamed would be possible!"

Potential Functions for This Tip: Teaching, Planning for the Future, Responding to Objections, Encouraging Students, Influencing Students, Resolving Conflicts

11. Can Do

We all like to hear what we can do, rather than what we cannot do. When someone tells us that we can't do something, we feel discouraged; when someone tells us what we *can* do, we feel encouraged. Use phrases such as "close," "good try," "you're on the right track," "you're getting there," "keep going," "you're almost there," and so on with your students. Try to avoid shaking your head, indicating "no," when you are responding to your students.

Students feel strong when you say, "Yes! That is correct," nod your head, and focus on the positive. Accentuating the positive helps you to feel stronger, too. The next time you are tempted to shake your head "no," find other words to say and nod "yes" instead. Both the student and you will be rewarded.

- Instead of saying, "No, you can't do X," say, *"You can do Y."*
- Instead of saying, "No, you shouldn't do X," say, *"It might be helpful for you to do Y."*

- Instead of saying, "You are wrong," say, "*You are close*" or "*Here is the correct answer.*"

- Instead of saying, "That is a problem," say, "*That is an opportunity for us to do some creative thinking.*"

Potential Functions for This Tip: Building Relationships, Teaching, Planning for the Future, Responding to Objections, Encouraging Students, Influencing Students, Resolving Conflicts

12. Choices

We have all had experiences when someone told us what to do, and we didn't feel as though we had any choice in the matter. How do you feel in that type of situation? Not great! We all want to have choices in what we do.

Dreikurs and Grey (1968) discuss the importance of giving students choices. The more choices we can give them, the more they will feel in control. The more they feel in control, the less they will need to try to gain control from us.

Fay and Funk (1995) suggest giving students two choices (or more, depending on the age of the students), "either of which would make you [the adult] deliriously happy" (p. 30). They emphasize letting students choose between several choices in order to give them a "say" in what concerns them. For example, when you give assignments, you could invite students to choose which assignment to do or how to present the information.

Many teachers use Gardner's (2006) multiple intelligences theory to give students choices as to how they will present their projects. Some students might choose to write music (musical intelligence), while others might choose to represent their work graphically (spatial intelligence), and so on. Here are some ways to emphasize student choice:

- "You have two choices for doing this assignment. The first one is to do X, and the second one is to do Y. Which might you prefer?"

• "Do you prefer to turn in your work before you wash your hands for lunch or after you wash your hands for lunch?"

• "Would you like to go to recess with your completed paper still on your desk or with your completed paper on my desk? Either way will be fine."

• "Would you like to work quietly at your desk or by my desk?"

You can also use language to convey to students that they made their own choices:

• "It looks like you chose to get into a fight when you were on the playground."

• "You appear to have decided to hand in your homework three days late."

In addition, you can use words to imply that students chose positive behaviors, conveying to them that they have the power to choose:

• "You have chosen to hand in your work on time every time that it is due."

• "When you are outside playing, you always choose to treat your friends with respect."

When students are stuck for ideas, you can also offer them a menu of items from which they can choose. According to B. Wellman (personal communication, September 1995), when you offer a student one choice, he or she may feel obliged to choose it or else risk offending you or harming your relationship. Offering two choices puts the student in a dilemma. Only when you offer three or more choices can the student truly be free to choose what might work best for him or her.

As you offer choices to students, gesture to the side to indicate where each of the choices lies. Look at your hand as you do so, rather than at students (Ellison, Hayes, Costa, & Garmston, 2008).

Students will follow your gaze, making the issue about the choices themselves, not about their relationship with you. Before offering the choices, you might first ask students if they would like to know what others have tried:

- "One possibility is W, another possibility is X, another possibility is Y, and another possibility is Z. What are some other possibilities that come to mind? Which of the possibilities could work for you?"
- "Some students have done A, other students have done B, other students have done C, and others have done D. What other options might you suggest? What are some of your thoughts as to what might work in this particular situation?"

Potential Functions for This Tip: Building Relationships, Teaching, Planning for the Future, Responding to Objections, Encouraging Students, Influencing Students, Resolving Conflicts

13. Choosing To

The words we choose to use can have a powerful impact on our experience. Jim Fay once told me that it doesn't matter whether what we tell our brains is true or not; the brain will always treat the information as being correct. We believe what we tell ourselves.

At times, students use words such as "have to," "must," and "need to." These words have different effects on different people. Some people use them to propel themselves toward completing something. Others react by moving away from what they want to do. Invite students to explore the words and see which ones most powerfully propel them toward doing a task.

When I tell myself, "I have to do this, "I need to do this," or "I must do this," I tend to react negatively. Other people may react positively. What helps propel me toward acting is saying, "I want to do this" or "I am choosing to do this." I may "need" to do it or "have to" do it, yet by saying that I want to do it and am choosing to do it, I am telling myself that I have choice in the matter.

Other people may be motivated by telling themselves, "I have to do this." If they merely choose to do it, they may not be moved to action. Only when things become serious and they are up against a deadline will they be spurred to action.

Ask students how each of the words makes them feel. Ask what they see, hear, and feel as they use the following phrases:

- "I *have* to do this."
- "I *need* to do this."
- "I *must* do this."
- "I *choose* to do this."
- "I *want* to do this."
- "I *would like* to do this."
- "It *would be fun* to do this."
- "It *will be fun* to do this."

Finally, invite them to choose what they say to themselves.

Potential Functions for This Tip: Planning for the Future, Responding to Objections, Encouraging Students

14. Consciously Noticing

Every moment of every day, we continually perceive things. We have so many things to notice in our environment that if we were to notice every detail, we would have no time to do anything else. Our minds work on many levels, both conscious and unconscious. By asking, "Have you *consciously* noticed something," we imply that students can notice both consciously and unconsciously. We can bring resources and successes to students' minds that they had previously noticed, but not consciously (Hall, 2004). We might ask them questions like the following:

- "Have you *consciously* noticed your developing potential and limitless resources yet?"
- "Have you *consciously* noticed from time to time just how powerfully and rapidly you are progressing toward your goals?"

- "Have you *consciously* been aware of your increasing potential in a multitude of areas?"
- "Have you *consciously* noticed all of the incredible things that you are learning each day?"
- "Have you *consciously* been aware of all of the skills that you are incorporating into the project that you and your friends are preparing?"

Potential Functions for This Tip: Responding to Objections, Encouraging Students, Influencing Students, Resolving Conflicts

15. Contexts

Students don't always do what we would prefer for them to do; however, sometimes it's just a matter of finding a more appropriate context for their behavior, according to Dilts and DeLozier (2000). We can ask the learners in what contexts their behavior might be appropriate. We can also affirm that other contexts exist in which that behavior might be completely appropriate.

Consider fighting. People pay a lot of money to see prizefighters in a ring, so fighting is appropriate in that context. In addition, if someone is attacked, fighting may be the only way to stay alive. By keeping this in mind, we can show learners that their behavior can be appropriate and even valuable in another context.

- "In what other *contexts* might procrastinating be the very best thing to do?"
- "What are some *contexts* in which that behavior could be the right thing to do?"
- "What might be some more appropriate *contexts* for that behavior?"
- "If you were a prizefighter, those behaviors would be extremely appropriate."

Potential Functions for This Tip: Teaching, Responding to Objections, Encouraging Students, Influencing Students, Resolving Conflicts

16. Continuing

We can assist learners in connecting what they are learning with what they have learned before, as well as what they will learn in the future (Hall, 2004). What is your reaction when someone says, "We are going to start our lesson now"? You may envision the beginning of a lesson.

In reality, today's lesson is a continuance of the many lessons that have gone before and a precursor to future lessons. If you rephrase the statement—"We are going to continue our lesson now"—you communicate that concept to students. See the following examples:

- "We will be *continuing* to learn about decimals today."
- "As we *continue* our journey of learning fractions, what are some of the questions that have arisen since yesterday?"
- "We are *continuing* our study of astronauts."

Potential Functions for This Tip: Teaching, Planning for the Future, Encouraging Students, Resolving Conflicts

17. Counterexamples

Have you ever focused so intently on what you had perceived as a problem that you dismissed the counter-examples from your mind? You saw only the problem but didn't see the many examples that indicated that no problem existed.

According to Dr. Christina Hall, when learners perceive something as a problem, they focus on a snapshot of an ongoing process (C. Hall, personal communication, June 2006). Finding a counterexample for them can loosen their stranglehold on that portrayal of the situation. The following statements are examples:

- "I procrastinate."
- ○ "You told me that *quickly!*"

- "I am not motivated."
- "You were *motivated* to tell me that!"
- "I have never succeeded in anything!"
- "You *succeeded* in telling me that!"
- "I can't write."
- "Really? Then who *wrote* the last assignment that you turned in to me?
- "I can't concentrate."
- "You are certainly *concentrating* on talking with me right now!"

Potential Functions for This Tip: Responding to Objections, Encouraging Students, Influencing Students, Resolving Conflicts

18. "Create for Yourself . . ."

We are completely in charge of creating the kind of life that we want for ourselves. We can invite students to create things for themselves, as well. By doing so, we encourage their creativity, and we invite them to open new horizons for themselves.

- "*Create for yourself* the life that you have always imagined yet never dreamed that you could have."
- "*Create for yourself* the successes in school and ultimately in life that make you feel really pleased and proud of yourself and your accomplishments!"
- "*Create for yourself* the learnings and insights that you have always wanted to have."
- "*Create for yourself* the kind of reputation that brings a smile to your face."
- "*Create for yourself* the friends who will be your friends for the rest of your life."

Potential Functions for This Tip: Teaching, Planning for the Future, Encouraging Students, Influencing Students, Resolving Conflicts

19. Curious

I was recently at the doctor's office to address a physical problem that had been lessened during the previous summer, when I was swimming regularly. My doctor wisely said, "I am curious to know just how quickly you will eliminate the problem by swimming again." Case closed—I began swimming right away!

Are you curious to know the short-term and long-term effects of using the language tips with your students? You can use the word "curious" to imply that your students will be doing certain things:

- "I will be *curious* to see just how quickly you complete this assignment."
- "I'll be *curious* to know your reactions to what you are reading."
- "I will be *curious* to hear your thoughts about the material in this unit."

Potential Functions for This Tip: Teaching, Planning for the Future, Responding to Objections, Encouraging Students, Influencing Students, Resolving Conflicts

20. Denominalizing

Turning verbs into nouns by adding endings such as "-ship," "-tion," "-sion," and so on creates "nominalizations." Verbs imply movement, yet nouns are stuck in time. Examples of nominalizations include "relationship" (vs. relating), "friendship" (vs. making friends), and "interaction" (vs. interacting). What do you visualize when you hear the word "relationship"? What do you visualize when you hear the word "relating"?

By turning the nominalizations back into verbs that end in "-ing" (denominalizing), we can help students put movement back into what they are saying so that they are visualizing an ongoing process rather than a moment that is stuck in time. This is one step toward helping students to see learning and all of life as an ongoing process (Hall, 2004).

Ellerbrœk (1978) called attention to the fact that in the field of medicine, names of diseases are nouns, such as cancer, epilepsy, measles, heart disease, and tumors. When people have a disease, the process of the disease, including healing, is not built into the word that defines the disease. He suggested that if diseases ended with "-ing"—"measling," for example—people may see them as being processes (p. 35). Some examples of denominalizing follow:

- "I have a good *relationship* with my friend." (a snapshot of a point in time)
  ○ "So you are *relating* well with your friend." (a process)
- "I have *friendships* with people in this class."
  ○ "So you are using your skills at *making friends* with people in this class."
- "I had positive *interactions* with other students in the class."
  ○ "So you and your colleagues were *interacting* positively."

Potential Functions for This Tip: Teaching, Planning for the Future, Responding to Objections, Encouraging Students, Influencing Students, Resolving Conflicts

21. Do It—Don't Try to Do It

The little word "try" conveys a powerful presupposition. What does "I'll try to do it" really mean? Maybe the person will do it, and maybe not.

What comes to mind when someone says, "I will do it"? We believe that they will do everything in their power to accomplish the task.

When students say, "I'll try to do it," ask, "What happens when you say, 'I'll do it'?" Share this tip with students to help them to accomplish their goals. You might demonstrate it by putting a pen on the floor and asking students to "try to pick it up" and see what happens.

Potential Functions for This Tip: Teaching, Planning for the Future, Responding to Objections, Encouraging Students, Influencing Students, Resolving Conflicts

22. "Don't . . . Unless You Really Want To . . ."

You can use negative words to your advantage by saying things such as, "Don't study unless you really want to do well in this class." This plays to the negativity that some students embrace. The last part of the message is what the student hears and remembers. You can also emphasize the last part of the sentence with your voice:

- *"Don't* study *unless you really want to do well in this class."*
- *"Don't* come to class *unless you want to learn everything that you possibly can about the topic to enable you to achieve your dreams."*
- *"Don't* think about your higher purposes for learning this material *unless you want to benefit many people."*
- *"Don't* ask questions about things you are not yet sure of *unless you want to truly understand and internalize the material."*
- *"Don't* share what you are learning with your friends and family *unless you want to learn things at even deeper levels."*

Potential Functions for This Tip: Teaching, Planning for the Future, Responding to Objections, Encouraging Students, Influencing Students, Resolving Conflicts

23. Eliminating "I"

When someone says, "I want you to do this," what is your first reaction? You may want to push the idea away. As self-directed people, we want to make the choices about our activities, yet, if that person were to ask, "Might it be possible for you to do this?" you might be more inclined to act on the suggestion. When teachers use the word "I," the focus is on the teacher rather than on the students. We have all heard teachers make statements like the following:

- "I want you to walk on the playground."
- "I want you to come when the bell rings."
- "I want you to turn in your assignment."

In the mid-1990s, I visited numerous classrooms with Michael Grinder to examine classroom management techniques. When he heard teachers using the word "I" a lot, he started tallying the number of times that they used the word. When he met with them to provide feedback, he suggested that the next time they were tempted to use the word "I," they could substitute the word "by":

- "*By* walking on the playground, you will be able to . . ."
- "*By* coming when the bell rings, you will be able to . . ."
- "*By* turning in your assignment, you will be able to . . ."

Potential Functions for This Tip: Building Relationships, Teaching, Planning for the Future, Responding to Objections, Encouraging Students, Influencing Students, Resolving Conflicts

24. Embedding Suggestions

When you want students to do something that they might resist if you asked them directly, you can embed suggestions into your language so that students aren't aware that they are being asked to do something. Emphasize the suggestion with your intonation.

- "When you use your new learnings, you will be surprised and delighted at just how quickly your life is changing in new and wonderful ways."
- "As you participate in the exercises, you will make many new and exciting discoveries that you hadn't yet thought about that will enrich your life and many other lives."
- "I'm sure that you will agree with me that these concepts and skills are really exciting and have the potential to open up many opportunities for you and for others around you."

• "You'll be amazed at just how quickly you learn the concepts and strategies that we will discuss."

• "Are you curious yet to know and understand all of the material behind the content that we are studying?"

Potential Functions for This Tip: Teaching, Responding to Objections, Encouraging Students, Influencing Students, Resolving Conflicts

25. "Even Better"

Has anyone ever told you, "That is better than it was before"? How did you feel? You may have felt a little bit discouraged because you had worked hard and didn't think that it was quite that bad before! What if they had said, "That is *even better* than it was before"? What impact might that have had on your reaction?

The tiny word "even" can pack a powerful punch. After I had cleaned a room and reorganized it, my husband used to say, "This room looks much better!" That felt like a put-down, as it implied that the room didn't look good before then. If he said, "The room looks *even* better," he would be implying that the room looked good before and that it looks even better now.

"You are doing better" implies that the person was not doing well prior to now. "You are doing *even* better" communicates that the student was already doing well and is now improving (Andreas, 1992).

• "This assignment is *even better* than the last one you turned in."

• "I bet you feel *even better* after having finished this!"

• "This assignment is *even longer* than the last one."

• "It looks like you worked *even harder* than you did on the last assignment."

• "You did *even better* on your spelling test this week than last week."

Potential Functions for This Tip: Building Relationships, Teaching, Planning for the Future, Responding to Objections, Encouraging Students, Influencing Students, Resolving Conflicts

26. Feedback

We have all received feedback on our work. Some feedback leaves us somewhat discouraged. Other feedback makes us feel strong. What are the differing characteristics of feedback that lead to such disparate results?

Ellison and colleagues (2008) identify five types of feedback: making judgments, providing information about the person who is giving feedback, making inferences, providing data, and asking reflective questions. When we use the first three types of feedback with students, we take away their ability to judge their own work.

Making Judgments

It is helpful to stay completely away from making judgments, both positive and negative, about student work or other issues related to students (Ellison et al., 2008). Even if we make positive judgments such as "Your work is good" or "You did a great job," students know that if we can make positive judgments, we can also make negative judgments. In addition, if we tell one student "Good job" in front of the class, other students might feel slighted if we neglect to say it to them. If we say "Good job" to a student one time, the student might feel slighted if we don't say it every time the student does something.

When we make judgments about student work, we put ourselves above the students. We also teach students to look for affirmation and judgment from outside of themselves, rather than from within (Fay & Funk, 1995), and that the opinions of others are more important than their own self-assessment. Thus, it is helpful to avoid making judgments at all costs. Examples of phrases to avoid include the following:

- "You did well."
- "That was a good report."
- "That was excellent."
- "You did a poor job on that."

Providing Information About the Person Who Is Giving Feedback

The second type of feedback is information about the person who is giving the feedback. The words "I," "me," "us," or derivations of those words are present in this type of feedback. Ellison and colleagues (2008) suggest avoiding this type of feedback as well. As with judgments, the following statements suggest that the opinion of the person giving the feedback is more important than the thoughts and feelings of the person who is doing the work and eliminate the opportunity for students to judge their own work:

- "I enjoyed your presentation."
- "I liked the way you entered the room."
- "It pleased me to see the work that you did."

Making Inferences

Inferences are conclusions that people draw from data. Two people can view the same data and draw different conclusions. Ellison and colleagues (2008) suggest that we avoid making inferences like the following:

- "You moved around a lot during the presentation. You must have been nervous."
- "You used a lot of authors in your report. You must have worked really hard."
- "You went to a lot of trouble in putting together the final project."

The final two types of feedback, providing data and asking reflective questions, help students learn to assess themselves.

Providing Data

Ellison and colleagues (2008) suggest that students benefit when we provide them with data that nobody could dispute. Using these data, students can make their own judgments and inferences.

- "You stood in five different spots during the five minutes that you were presenting to the group."
- "You cited 48 authors in the report that you turned in."
- "You said that you spent a total of 60 hours preparing the final project."

Asking Reflective Questions

According to Ellison and colleagues (2008), after providing students with data, we should ask reflective questions to guide them in thinking about and processing the data. In response to the data above, we might ask the following reflective questions:

- "You stood in five different spots during the five minutes that you were presenting to the group. What were some of the things that you were seeking to communicate with the audience from each of the different spots?
- "You cited 48 authors in the report that you turned in. What were some of the strategies that you used to obtain and read that many authors?"
- "You said that you spent a total of 60 hours preparing the final project. What were some of the strategies that you used to focus on the project in order to complete it?"

Potential Functions for This Tip: Teaching, Encouraging Students, Influencing Students

27. Feeling Smart

Sometimes when we are introduced to a new concept that we know nothing about, we feel less than smart. Since we all know—and dread—that feeling, we would do well to find ways to help our students feel smart, even when they are learning new material. Bob Garmston shared that one way is to "pre-teach" new concepts to students so that when we are ready to formally teach them, students will already have some knowledge about the topic and feel smart.

How can you put this technique into practice? You can talk about the concept and go through the key points that students need to know in order to understand it either at the beginning of the day or the day before you actually teach the topic. You might say, "Tomorrow (or later today), we will be talking about _____. We will be doing exercises on the topic. An example is _____. Here is another example. Another example is _____. If you would like to read a little bit in advance, you can turn to page _____." You could also invite students to talk with their parents about the topic that night.

Another strategy for pre-teaching is to point out to students that they have already had experiences with the topic before. When teaching students to tell time, you could say, "How many of you have seen a clock? How many of you have wondered what the hands meant? Perhaps you have asked your parents what time it was. Perhaps your parents have explained a little bit to you about what the two hands on a clock mean and how to determine what time it is."

To teach students about fractions, you could start by saying, "We are going to be talking about fractions today. Perhaps you have wanted to share a candy bar with a friend. How did you determine where to cut the candy bar? Perhaps your mother has made a pie and wanted to cut it so that everyone in the family had an equal piece. What does 'equal' mean? How did she determine where to cut the pieces?"

Potential Functions for This Tip: Teaching, Encouraging Students

28. Flipping It

Sometimes students say that they want to do something yet place a restriction on it: "I want to do the assignment, but I don't have time." You can address this circumstance by "flipping it" in order to reinforce their motivation or desire. The brain tends to negate what comes after the word "but"; however, by turning it around, you can honor and validate what the student wants to do (Hall, 2004). In the student statements below, students are focusing on what is getting in the way of what they want to do. By flipping the statements, you can help them remember what they want to do. You can also put the first clause into past tense.

- "I want to do this assignment, but I am tired."
- "So you said that you were tired, but you want to *do this assignment*."
- "I want to come to class, but I have a lot going on."
- "So you have had a lot going on, but you want to *come to class*."
- "I want to take this class, but my mother is sick.
- "So your mother has been sick, but you want to *take this class*."

Potential Functions for This Tip: Responding to Objections, Influencing Students, Resolving Conflicts

29. Future Pacing

How did we learn to see the future? People pointed it out to us, didn't they? They helped us to visualize it, and they helped us to see what we could become.

My parents told me when I was growing up that I could be a concert pianist, a teacher, or a nurse. What a surprise! I became a teacher. I didn't like blood, so that ruled out nursing. I had to practice the piano every day for an hour, which was a negative factor for me. Ultimately, I chose teaching as a career. Whether consciously or unconsciously, my parents helped me to visualize the future and plan for it.

When you talk with students, add a sentence or two to imply that they will be successful in the future. By doing so, you express your belief in their value and worth. You also help them to visualize the future and plan for it.

- "Wow! You are really a hard worker! My guess is that you will experience a lot of success next year in 3rd grade, as well as every year in the future!"
- "You are going to succeed beyond your wildest dreams, both next year and many years into the future. You will definitely earn several degrees in higher education!"
- "In the future, I can see you as a highly successful doctor" (lawyer, teacher, businessperson, dancer, singer, artist, etc.).
- "What are some of your goals and dreams for yourself at the university and beyond? What are some of the subjects that you will study first?"

Going into the Future, Now Looking Back . . .

Another motivating strategy for helping students to visualize the future is to invite them to go into the future, and then look back at what they did to accomplish their goals (Hall, 2006). This process can help students to see the steps that they took to succeed.

- "After you have completed this project and are looking back, what was the first step that you took in the process of completing it?"
- "Moving into the future and looking back, having already finished the course with a grade of *A,* what were some of the things that you did to accomplish it?"
- "When you have completed your degree, looking back, what were some of the tasks that you did that helped you to be successful?"

Past, Present, and Future

When students are "stuck," they are labeling something that they perceive as a limitation that keeps them from accomplishing something that they value (Hall, 2006). They are not focusing on the many resources that they have available to them, both internal and external, nor are they seeing themselves as being successful in the future. According to Hall, we can use verb tenses to help learners put a limitation in the past, add a resource in the present, and visualize success in the future.

- "So you *had* trouble until now with that (past), and you *are applying* your new learnings and strategies to learn it (present resources) so that you *will succeed* in that area in the future (future success)."
- "You *had perceived* that as a problem (past), and with all of the methods you *are gaining* (present resources), you *will succeed* in the future (future success)."
- "You *had thought* that that was a problem (past) until you realized all of the resources that you *have* now, both internally and externally (present resources), are enabling you to *move forward* toward achieving your dreams beyond your wildest expectations (future success)."

Looking Forward, Looking Back . . . and Looking Forward Again

When we feel "stuck" in the present, we can have difficulty seeing the future. You can help students to see their lives on a continuum with your language (Hall, 2006). First, invite students to look forward into the future:

- "What are some of the ideas that you have now for accomplishing your goal?"
- "What are some of the strategies that you will use in the process of accomplishing your goal?"

Then invite them to look back, seeing what they have already done. Perhaps they can even walk into the future, turn around, and look back at the present:

- "Going into the future now and looking back, having already accomplished all that you were wanting to accomplish and even more, what were some of the strategies that you used in the process of accomplishing your goals?"

• "Going into the future now and looking back, having accomplished more than you ever imagined possible, what were some of the steps that you took in the process of moving forward rapidly?"

Finally, invite them to come back to the present and look forward, seeing the path that they will take toward achieving their goal:

• "Now, coming back into the present, what are some of the next steps that you will take in the process of completing the paper?"
• "Now, returning to the present and looking forward to all that you will accomplish, what are some of the emotions that you feel as you move forward more quickly than you ever dreamed possible?"

Potential Functions for This Tip: Teaching, Planning for the Future, Responding to Objections, Encouraging Students, Influencing Students, Resolving Conflicts

30. Green Elephants

How would you react if someone said to you, "Don't think of green elephants"? What would you immediately think of? You would obviously form a picture of green elephants in your mind in order to process the request (Hall, 2006). You might even continue thinking about green elephants.

How many times have we heard teachers say, "Don't use a crayon," "Don't run," or "Don't hit people on the playground." Students' brains remember what they hear, yet they delete the "don't." Thus, students remember "Use a crayon," "Run," and "Hit people on the playground." Teachers then wonder why students do exactly what they were asked not to do. "Didn't I tell you not to use a crayon?" Students were just doing what we put into their minds. Some people who see a sign saying, "Don't walk on the grass," might find themselves thinking, "That would never have occurred to me.

Now that you mention it, it seems like a good idea!" When you talk with students, tell them what you *want* them to do!

- "Please treat people with respect."
- "Please keep your hands to yourself."
- "Please walk in the hallways."

You can also ask students to "remember to do X" rather than saying, "don't forget."

- Instead of saying: "Don't forget to turn off the lights,"
- ○ Say: "*Remember* to turn off the lights."
- Instead of saying: "Don't forget to walk,"
- ○ Say: "*Be sure* to walk."
- Instead of saying: "Don't forget to do your homework,"
- ○ Say: "*Please remember* to do your homework."

Grinder (personal communication, April 2009) suggests three considerations for positive and negative statements. If a person is doing something for the first time, we can just state the positive. If the person has done it inappropriately before, we can use the negative and follow it with the positive. If the person is slow to grasp what we are asking him or her to do, we can use the positive, then the negative, and then the positive. The key is to always end with the positive statement.

Potential Functions for This Tip: Teaching, Planning for the Future, Encouraging Students, Influencing Students, Resolving Conflicts

31. High Expectations

Ladson-Billings (1994) found that in order for students to achieve at high levels, teachers must communicate to the students that they have high expectations for them. When teachers believe that students can achieve, they do (see also Armor et al., 1976; Newman,

1993; Tracz & Gibson, 1986). Ladson-Billings recounted a powerful story about her 5th grade teacher, "the teacher who I think is most responsible for my belief that some teachers truly motivate students to be their very best" (p. 18). She said that this teacher, Mrs. Benn, "demanded excellence at every task we undertook. We were required to write with precise handwriting and perfect spelling. . . . She warned us that playing around in her class meant that we did not value ourselves. 'This is your chance, don't let it slip away,' she urged" (p. 19).

Grinder (2005) suggests that by standing tall at the front of the classroom with toes straight ahead and our weight balanced evenly on both feet, we are communicating high expectations. He also suggests having our forearms either down to the side of our bodies or bent at the waist and parallel to the ground. We could also have a combination of one forearm down to the side and the other parallel to the ground (M. Grinder, personal communication, September 1995). As we stand tall in front of the class, we communicate to students that we expect the best from them.

We can also use language to communicate our high expectations:

- "As you learn more and more every day, you must really feel great about all that you are accomplishing!"
- "Even though this seems a little bit difficult right now, you will be surprised and delighted at just how quickly you have mastered it!"
- "I am sure that you are noticing just how rapidly you are incorporating this new material into your already growing and expanding repertoire!"
- "As we learn this material, you will use all of the strategies that you have been using all along to master everything that you are learning!"

Potential Functions for This Tip: Building Relationships, Teaching, Planning for the Future, Responding to Objections, Encouraging Students, Influencing Students, Resolving Conflicts

32. "How . . . ?"

How can we make each day the most powerful day in the lives of our students? How can we help them to remember this day many years from now, as they think back on the education that they received? How can we show them just how much potential they really have to make the kind of impact on the world that they want to make?

According to O'Connor and Seymour (1990), " 'How' questions will get you an understanding of the structure of a problem. 'Why' questions are likely to get you justifications and reasons without changing anything" (p. 5). The tiny word "how," when used at the beginning of a question, can open up many possibilities for students.

- "*How* does knowing this affect your life?"
- "*How* does having already completed your assignments make you feel pleased about the ways in which you are progressing toward your goals?"
- "*How* might you be able to complete this assignment quickly and joyfully?"
- "*How* might you be learning everything that you possibly can in the process of moving toward fulfilling your missions?"
- "*How* can understanding these principles help you in your future career and beyond?"
- "*How* might you use the study habits that you are learning at the university?"

Potential Functions for This Tip: Teaching, Planning for the Future, Responding to Objections, Encouraging Students, Influencing Students, Resolving Conflicts

33. "I Apologize" Versus "I'm Sorry"

Some people continually say, "I'm sorry." They almost seem as though they are apologizing for being. In some cases, the phrase "I'm sorry" can appear to communicate that the person is sorry at the identity level: "I am a sorry person."

If you were to ask someone to hold out his or her arm and push up, while you pushed down on the arm, and then ask the person to say, "I'm sorry," the arm would go weak. If instead you asked the person to say, "I apologize," the arm would remain strong, indicating that the person felt strong. Strange as it seems, when we say, "I apologize," we are making ourselves feel strong; when we say, "I'm sorry," we are making ourselves feel weak.

If a student is going to apologize to another student, it is preferable for the student to say "I apologize" than to say "I'm sorry." It is also helpful if students decide that it is right for them to apologize, rather than asking (or forcing) them to apologize when they do not feel like they want to do so.

Potential Functions for This Tip: Responding to Objections, Resolving Conflicts

34. "I Will . . ."

We have all had times when we asked people to do something and they refused. We can certainly understand. Still, the manner in which they refused may have either been acceptable or caused us to feel somewhat badly about having asked them and wish we hadn't asked.

Rather than telling students what you won't do, tell them what you will do. It is also helpful to smile at the same time. Rather than asking students to be quiet or saying that you won't begin class until students are quiet, you might say (with a smile), "We will begin class when the room is quiet." If some students tend to be late in turning in assignments, you might say, "All assignments that are in my box by 3 p.m. today will receive a grade." If some students tend not to get their books out, you might say, "We will be discussing the material on page 50."

When I started giving seminars in Mexico, people would ask me to do various things for them. My immediate response was to think of the extra burden that it would add for me and to say, "No." A Mexican friend taught me that the correct response was, "¿Como no?" This means, "Why not?" in Spanish. The suggestion is to adopt a "why not" attitude when responding to students.

By telling students what we will do instead of what we won't do, we create positive relationships. Words such as "happy" and "glad to" also help convey a positive message to students.

- "I will be glad to look at that when you have finished."
- "I will be happy to work with you sometime next week after class."
- "Students who are quiet will be dismissed."
- "Students who are working quietly will receive a happy face."

You can also ask students to say what they will be doing rather than what they will not be doing to help them to focus on positive behaviors. By using the "-ing" ending, you can help them to see their task as an ongoing process.

In the past, educators used to ask students to write 100 sentences regarding what they would not do, such as "I will not hit people" or "I will not throw things." Those educators were imprinting the negative behaviors on the students' minds without knowing it. After writing the negative statements so many times, students were probably more likely to engage in the exact behaviors that the well-intentioned educators were seeking to eliminate. Try rephrasing such sentences in a positive way:

- Rather than saying, "I won't hit people," students can say, "I will keep my hands to myself" or "I will treat others respectfully."
- Rather than saying, "I won't run," students can say, "I will walk."
- Rather than saying, "I won't play around in class," students can say, "I will do my work in class."

Potential Functions for This Tip: Building Relationships, Teaching, Planning for the Future, Influencing Students, Resolving Conflicts

35. Identities

We tend to behave according to the way we see ourselves. If you perceive your identity as that of a responsible worker, you will be a responsible worker. Dilts (1999) developed a schematic called the Neuro-Logical Levels based on the work of Bateson (1972). We can use this schema to instill positive identities in our students.

Spiritual or Mission

This is the higher purpose for doing something. People talk of serving God, changing the world, bringing peace, and so on; we are always doing things for a higher purpose. We can help students focus on their higher purposes for doing what they are doing. Students of all ages can get involved in raising money to help children in other countries, doing volunteer work, and performing other charitable acts.

Identity

Our identity is who we are. People often use the words "I am" to describe themselves. We have many identities in life: mother, father, child, parent, successful person, teacher, principal, student, learner, physically fit person, happy person, and so on. When we say "I am," we are talking about identity. Generally, identity is fixed.

People often freeze an ongoing process of identity formation by taking a snapshot of themselves in a particular situation and labeling it (Hall, 2006). One person may have had a period of time in which he or she was doing something in a way that looked disorganized. He or she might take a mental snapshot of time and say, "I am disorganized," placing the perceived ongoing process of disorganization at the identity level. A student may have experienced a time of not being able to read as well as other classmates could read, take a snapshot of that, and conclude (at the identity level) that "I'm dumb" or "I'm not a reader."

Students form many beliefs about themselves based on generalizations they have made in their lives, and they tend to act based on their identities in a situation. Students who have identities such as "I am a good student," "I am helpful," "I am responsible," "I am smart," "I am an athlete," "I am a good football player," "I am a hard worker," "I am a writer," and "I am a reader" tend to behave accordingly. On the other hand, students who have formed negative identities either by being told by important people in their lives that they are a certain way or by generalizing based on their experiences will tend to react in negative ways. Negative identities include "I am bad," "I am a poor student," "I am a troublemaker," "I am not athletic," "I am not good enough," "I am shy," "I am not artistic," "I am a failure," "I am clumsy," "I am dumb," and so on.

We are in a special position to help instill positive identities in every student we meet. We can continually search for opportunities to find students doing positive things and say, "You are _____" in order to instill positive identities in them. What are some positive identities that you can give to students with whom you are associated?

Beliefs and Values

Beliefs and values are concepts that we hold to be true. We may believe that education is important and value learning. We may believe that we cannot succeed. We may believe certain things about how schools should operate. We may have certain spiritual beliefs. Students may believe that they can succeed or that they cannot succeed. They may value school, or they may not value it. They may value their friendships, their toys, their motorcycle, or other things. They may hold certain spiritual beliefs. We can help students to believe that they can achieve what they want to achieve and value learning and becoming what they want to become. We can also assist them in changing negative beliefs into positive beliefs.

Capabilities

Capabilities are clusters of behaviors that we can perform. We can teach students to read, send e-mail, compose a letter, use a computer, select clothes to wear for the day, write a paper, and so on.

Students' capabilities include reading, writing a story, doing mathematical problems and scientific experiments, reading a map, playing a sport, singing a song, playing an instrument, and so on.

Behaviors

Behaviors are the discrete actions that make up a capability. In teaching a child to read (a capability), we may say, "This is the letter 'a,' and it says, 'a.'" In teaching students to use a computer, we may say, "Hit the 'h' key."

Environment

We spend time in many environments—home, office, car, nature, and so on. Students also spend time in many environments—home, classroom, car, friends' houses, stores, and so on.

Applications

So, how do we use these Neuro-Logical Levels to help students achieve? We can take negative things that students have done and put them at the lower levels of behaviors and capabilities, and we can take positive things that students do and raise them to the level of identity. The following are examples of lowering the level:

• If a student gets angry, we might say, "You *had feelings* of anger because of this situation" (environment) rather than saying, "You *are* angry" (identity).

• If a student says, "I am not a public speaker" (identity), we might say, "You *have not yet learned* the skills to feel comfortable in front of a group" (capability).

• If a student says, "I *am* dumb because I didn't pass the test" (identity), we might say, "You *hadn't yet learned* that because you didn't have a chance to study for the test" (capability).

On the other hand, we can raise the level of positive things that students do to identity.

• "You read a lot! You truly *are* a reader."

- "You worked hard on your writing assignment. You *are* definitely a writer."
- "You always come in with a smile on your face. You *are* a happy person."
- "You relate well with others. You *are* a friendly person."

Potential Functions for This Tip: Building Relationships, Teaching, Planning for the Future, Responding to Objections, Encouraging Students, Influencing Students, Resolving Conflicts

36. Important Ideas

We have all had instructors who said, "This is going to be on the test," "Be sure and write this down," "This is really important," and "You are going to need to remember this." What was the result? We wrote down the material and remembered it! In my Western Civilization course my freshman year at the university, I had an instructor who did just that—thank goodness! The book contained so many details, including dates, information about rulers, and other topics, that our instructor telling us what was important helped us to learn it in order to perform well on the test!

We can assist students in their learning by pointing out important ideas and concepts so that they will know what to pay attention to more than other things and will know what to study. Helpful phrases include the following:

- "This is important."
- "Please be sure and study this section."
- "This will be on the test."
- "This is a key point that is important to know in order to understand this material."
- "Everything that we will be talking about will be based on this concept."

Potential Functions for This Tip: Teaching

37. "In the Long Run"

When learners perceive something as a limitation, we can help them to visualize it over a longer span of time in order to show them that where they are is just one instant in a lifetime of experiences. When I took a yearlong course in chemistry in high school, I struggled. In order to keep my grades up, I spent many nights at the local university library reading chemistry books to help me understand the various concepts that the teacher was presenting.

When I went to the University of Tennessee, chemistry was the major freshman "flunk-out" course in the College of Home Economics. As a result of studying the chemistry textbooks at the university when I was in high school, I was able to do well, while many other students had difficulty with the course. In the long run, my perseverance in a difficult situation paid off.

When students express limitations, it is usually because they see themselves only in the present, rather than incorporating the past or the future. Use the phrase "in the long run" to help students visualize themselves over a longer span of time.

- "I am spending a lot of time learning this."
- o "How might that really be a gift *in the long run*?"
- "I can't do this yet."
- o "How might that be the very best thing *in the long run*?"
- "I am struggling to learn this."
- o "In what ways could that be the biggest benefit of all to you *in the long run*?"
  - "I am having difficulty."
  - o "What might be the benefits of that difficulty *in the long run*?"

Potential Functions for This Tip: Teaching, Planning for the Future, Responding to Objections, Encouraging Students, Influencing Students, Resolving Conflicts

38. "-ing" Words

When we use words that end with "-ing," we help our students to view what we are saying as an ongoing process; they can visualize a video, rather than individual snapshots. Picture the "Breaking News" banner on your local news channel. Somehow, it always sends a ripple down our backs: "Wow! This is happening right now. How will it end?" Some examples of ways to use words that end with "–ing" follow:

- "You *are working* hard now."
- "You *are studying* for the test."
- "You *are using* many strategies for learning."
- "Members of your group *are collaborating* effectively in order to complete your project."

When we say, "You have been doing this," we show the person that the action began in the past and continues in the present. Consider the following examples:

- "You *have been doing* this for quite a while, haven't you?"
- "You *have been succeeding* in your studies for many years."
- "You *have been studying* hard for this test."
- "You and members of your group *have been working* together harmoniously for the past two weeks."

Potential Functions for This Tip: Teaching, Planning for the Future, Responding to Objections, Encouraging Students, Influencing Students, Resolving Conflicts

39. Inquiring Rather Than Interrogating

We have been processing questions since we were very young. Our parents may have asked, "*Where* were you?" "*Who* were you with?" "*What* did you do?" "*Why* did you do that?" Questions such as these may have elicited a less than positive response from us.

What if the questions were more open-ended? "Tell me about your evening." "Who were some of the people that were most entertaining?" "What were some of the activities that were most enjoyable?" "Tell me your reasons for doing that." The two types of questions address the same topics. What differences do you notice between them?

Many students have learned that when adults ask them questions, they are probably looking for specific answers to questions. In other words, only one correct answer exists, and the students need to know what it is. In addition, the adults could be planning on using the information they obtain against the students. When we feel like we are being interrogated, we can have difficulty thinking (Ellison et al., 2008). Think about the differences between interrogatory questions and true inquiries, where the questioner wants to know what the person really thinks.

One difference is that when people interrogate others, their voice goes down at the end of the question; in contrast, inquiries rise in tone at the end of the question (Grinder, 2007). In addition, people who are interrogating tend to have a closed body posture (perhaps with arms crossed), while those who are inquiring might have a more open body posture (arms to the side or outstretched, perhaps with palms of the hands facing up).

Another difference is that when people interrogate, they ask pointed questions for which only one answer is possible; when they inquire, they ask questions that can have many different answers. When we ask students questions for which only one answer exists, they are likely to resist or become defensive. When we phrase our questions to imply that many answers could be possible, we are likely to get thoughtful, reflective responses. We can help our students to feel comfortable and think more clearly when we focus on inquiring rather than interrogating.

Potential Functions for This Tip: Building Relationships, Teaching, Responding to Objections, Resolving Conflicts

40. Instructions

We have all been in a class and become distracted by something else. Suddenly, we realized that the instructor had given the class a long set of directions, and we were lost! We had no idea what the instructor asked us to do. We may have felt embarrassed to ask what the instructor said because we weren't listening. Nothing was written on the board, so we didn't even have that as a backup!

According to Prusak and colleagues (2005), teachers should give short instructions to get students started on a task. Then they can assist individual students who may be having difficulty with a particular aspect of the project. They suggest that teachers who give long sets of instructions tend to lose the attention of their students. By shortening the instructions and limiting the number of sentences they use, teachers can increase the chances that the students are attending to the task.

Prusak and colleagues (2005), as well as Grinder (2005), suggest that when giving instructions, teachers should use both verbal and nonverbal methods. By both saying and demonstrating what students should do, teachers can send 100 percent of the message.

Grinder (2005) gives the example of teachers saying, "Please raise your hand" while raising their hand themselves, thus indicating both verbally and nonverbally what they want students to do. When students become accustomed to raising their hands, teachers can just raise their hand to direct students. If students begin talking out, teachers can return to giving both the verbal and nonverbal message until students are again accustomed to raising their hands.

Grinder (2005) also suggests that, in addition to giving instructions verbally, teachers should write the instructions on the board, on a PowerPoint slide, or on a whiteboard to provide support for both auditory and visual learners. This practice saves learners from having to ask what they are supposed to do. How many times have we heard teachers saying in a somewhat exasperated tone of voice, "I just told you what to do!" As adults, do we always listen to what instructors are saying? By writing instructions on the board, we can enable students to spend more time on task, resulting in even greater learning.

Potential Functions for This Tip: Teaching

41. "It Is," "It Was"

We can imply that what we are saying is the truth by using "it is" and "it was."

- *"It is* wonderful to see you again."
- *"It was* really exciting to read the paper that you wrote."
- *"It is* so good to see you feeling so pleased with the work that you are producing."
- *"It was* fabulous looking at your papers."
- *"It is* great seeing you so happy today."
- *"It was* fun attending the game on Saturday night and seeing our team win!"

Potential Functions for This Tip: Building Relationships, Teaching, Responding to Objections, Encouraging Students

42. "It's Really About . . ."

Have you ever been so close to a situation that you didn't see what it was really about? Sometimes, students need to be reminded of their primary focus. They are thinking in terms of smaller things. We can help them to realize what is really important to them and others. We can label the concept that they are talking about to help give them a broader view.

- "So *it's really about* turning in quality work, isn't it?"
- "Safety on the playground is what is *really important* here."
- "Ensuring that all students feel safe in the classroom is *what we all want,* isn't it?"

- "Building satisfying relationships with others is *one of the most important things in life,* isn't it?"
- "Feeling good about what we turn in is *what we all want,* isn't it?"
- "*What is really important* is growing as learners and truly knowing that we can do anything we set our minds to do, isn't it?"

Potential Functions for This Tip: Responding to Objections, Encouraging Students, Influencing Students, Resolving Conflicts

43. "Know Best"

M. Grinder (personal communication, September 1996) taught me the magic of the four little words: "You would know best." When we say them to people, we show that we value their opinions and their perspectives. Every time I have said them, the person to whom I said them has smiled broadly. We are telling them that they would know best how to apply the material, how to use what they are learning, and how to proceed in various areas of their lives.

- "*You would know best* how to apply this in your professional life."
- "*You would know best* how to go about preparing your project."
- "*You would know best* which colleagues to choose to work with you."
- "*You would know best* what you would like to learn in this unit."
- "*You would know best* the strategies that will most powerfully help you in advancing toward your goals."

Potential Functions for This Tip: Building Relationships, Teaching, Planning for the Future, Responding to Objections, Encouraging Students, Influencing Students, Resolving Conflicts

44. Laughing

Nothing does the body good like an old-fashioned belly laugh! Cousins (2005) found that when people who had terminal illnesses watched comedy videos, their health improved. When we laugh with students, we build relationships, increase endorphins in our bodies, breathe deeply, and generally help ourselves feel better. Laughter truly is the best medicine, and we can share it with our students! Our students will remember the way we make them feel. If we are always serious, they will remember that. If we laugh with them a lot, they will remember that, as well.

When I was teaching 7th grade, I did a unit on stand-up comedy. Many of the students appeared to want to be stand-up comedians, so I thought that we might as well get some mileage from it! I read books by various comedians, shared their strategies with the students, and had students develop routines. Each day I invited one student to present a routine after lunch. In the book *Teaching Class Clowns (and What They Can Teach Us)* (Purkey, 2006), the author suggests ways to use the humor of class clowns for the benefit of all. Wanzer and Frymier (1999) found that "student perceptions of instructors' HO [humor orientation] were significantly and positively associated with student learning" (p. 57).

Numerous resources contain tips for laughing with students and using humor in the classroom. Why not begin each day with the *"Joke of the Day"*? Why not invite students to bring jokes to tell? (At certain grade levels, you may need to censor them first.) Why not intentionally build laughter—big belly laughs—into the school day?

Potential Functions for This Tip: Building Relationships, Teaching, Planning for the Future, Responding to Objections, Encouraging Students, Influencing Students, Resolving Conflicts

45. Linking Learning with Students' Lives

Culturally relevant educators ask questions to help students link what they know and are experiencing in their lives with what they are learning (Ladson-Billings, 1994). "These connections are made in spirited discussions and classroom interactions. Teachers are not afraid to assume oppositional viewpoints to foster the students' confidence in challenging what may be inaccurate or problematic" (Ladson-Billings, 1994, p. 94). Ann Lewis, a teacher in Ladson-Billings's study, invited students to draw a Venn diagram to illustrate the overlap between the lives of the characters in a story and the students' lives. She specifically asked the students, "How can you relate this to your life?" We might ask questions such as the following:

- "What are some of your experiences related to this topic?"
- "As you consider the ways that you interact with your friends, what are some of the possible applications that you can think of for what you are learning?"
- "What are some of the things that you observe in your daily life that relate to what we are discussing?"
- "As you think of your activities yesterday, how might they be related to this discussion?"
- "As you think of your family, what are some possible ways of applying what you are learning?"

Potential Functions for This Tip: Building Relationships, Teaching

46. Long-Term Consequences of Actions

As adults, we can often predict what might happen to students if they continue to think or behave in ways that have been unproductive in the past. Students cannot always see these consequences so easily. By taking them out into the future and looking back, we can drive the long-term consequences of their actions home to them even more powerfully.

A friend who is a coach did this for me in the area of weight loss. When we are in the present looking forward, it is easy to continue doing what we have done in the past. I would see food that I wanted, perhaps a piece of chocolate, tell myself that I could lose weight tomorrow, and eat it. While it is true that I could always lose weight beginning tomorrow, many years of doing this had not been helpful!

My friend took me into the future a year from now and helped me to look back having never made the decision, once and for all, to concentrate on losing weight for a period of time. AACCKKK! Then, she took me out five years into the future, having never made the decision to lose the weight. DOUBLE AACCKKK! Then, she took me out 10 years, 20 years, and to the end of my life, looking back, having never made the decision to lose the weight once and for all. The experience was so powerful that I began the diet that day and lost 25 pounds in record time!

We can help students see the long-term consequences of their actions if they continue to think or behave in the same way by stretching their behavior out to its logical conclusion.

- "If you were to continue for the rest of the semester without turning in assignments and coming to class, what might be some of the consequences?"
- "If you were to continue to avoid writing, what might happen to your dream of getting a higher degree?"
- "If you were to continue to hit people until you are 100 years old, what might be some of the results in terms of the number of friends you will have?"
- "If you were to continue to put your social life before your responsibilities, what might be some of the consequences that could possibly occur?"
- "What might happen if you avoided turning in assignments for the entire four years of your college career?"

Potential Functions for This Tip: Planning for the Future, Responding to Objections, Encouraging Students, Influencing Students, Resolving Conflicts

47. Magic Words

Many of us were raised to say the "magic words": "please" and "thank you." Those two little phrases can provide great benefits. Kuykendall (1993) discusses the importance of teachers modeling polite behavior with young children. Pianta developed an instrument to measure "three broad domains of supportive interactions: emotional support, organizational support, and instructional support" (*Harvard Education Letter*, 2008, para. 3). According to Pianta,

> Teachers who score high on positive emotional climate consistently demonstrate respect for their students. They are in proximity when they speak to the children in their classroom, establish eye contact before speaking to them, and address them by name. They consistently have a warm and calm tone and use language that communicates respect, such as saying "Please," "Thank you," and "You're welcome." The absence of harshness and tension is noticeable, and when conflicts arise they quickly dissipate. This type of environment is conducive to learning and allows children to feel safe to explore. (para. 3)

At the doctoral level, when I give feedback to students on their writing, instead of writing, "Do this," I am careful to write, "Please do this." I get positive responses from students when they receive my feedback, and I believe that a major reason is because of the word "please." I also say, "Thank you for sending your paper." I may add that it was a pleasure reading it and that they obviously put a lot of work into writing it (if that is true).

In what areas might you be able to say "please" and "thank you" as you work with your students? Consider the following:

- *"Please* turn in your assignments on time."
- *"Please* come to class prepared to discuss X."
- *"Please* be considerate of the people around you as you are working."

You can also say "thank you" either before learners do what you ask them to do or afterward. By thanking them afterward, you affirm that they did what you requested. By thanking them in advance for what they will be doing, you increase the chances that they will do it. In essence, you are presupposing that they will do it.

- *"Thank you* for turning your assignments in on time."
- *"Thank you* for keeping the classroom clean."
- *"Thank you* for pushing your chairs in."

Potential Functions for This Tip: Building Relationships, Teaching, Influencing Students, Resolving Conflicts

48. "Managing to . . ."

Sometimes in order to save face and preserve our self-esteem, we blame others for our difficulties or lack of perceived ability to do something. By placing the blame outside of ourselves, we are telling ourselves that the locus of control lies elsewhere, in other people.

When people perceive that they have limitations, they tend to believe that the control lies outside of themselves. If you ask them, "How do (or did) you manage to do X?" you presuppose that they have actually created the situation themselves. It follows, then, that they have the power and ability to change the situation by acting differently.

- "I can't complete my homework because I don't have time."
- ○ "How did you *manage to* create that situation?"
- "I can't come to class because I have conflicts."
- ○ "How did you *manage to* set up that situation?"
- "I don't think that I can do this."
- ○ "How did you *manage to* create that perception?"

Potential Functions for This Tip: Responding to Objections, Influencing Students, Resolving Conflicts

49. Meanings

As humans, we are meaning-making machines. We seek to attach meaning to events in order to make sense of them. Sometimes the meanings that we attach are helpful and productive, yet sometimes they are not.

For some reason, in the field of education, learners can get the idea that they are "failures" just because they didn't do as well as they had wanted in a class, because they hadn't taken the time to prepare, and so on. Instead of letting their attached meaning limit them, we can help students attach new meanings to a situation in order to open up possibilities.

- "I am a failure."
- "Just because you didn't have the time to study when your father was in the hospital that makes you a failure?"
- "I feel so bad because I didn't get the project done in time."
- "Because you have been putting the needs of others ahead of your own, benefiting others in a variety of ways, you haven't taken the time to do what was needed yet for completing this project?"
- "I can't do this."
- "Perhaps this means that you just haven't taken the time to learn to do it, or that you haven't taken advantage of the many people around you who would be happy to assist you in moving forward and understanding how to do it."
- "I can't stop thinking about everything that has happened in the past."
- "How can that be a gift that helps you to make meaning from the past in order to move forward in your life?"

Potential Functions for This Tip: Responding to Objections, Encouraging Students, Influencing Students, Resolving Conflicts

50. Metaphors

Have you ever had someone use a metaphor to describe a situation you were in that encouraged you and helped you to see the situation in a completely different way? Once, when I was experiencing a situation that I perceived as difficult, a friend said, "It's like you have been wandering in the forest with a thick growth of trees above, not able to *yet* see the bright sunshine and fluffy clouds above and feel the warmth of the air. As you are following the pathway out of the forest, what are some of the things that you are experiencing?" I felt great and found my way out of the situation rapidly after that!

In McCarthey's (1994) study, students who heard metaphors from their teacher spent time interpreting them and came to understand their meaning after engaging in discussions with the teacher. In addition, they used metaphors in their writing. Kilstein (1993) suggested that metaphors may enable students from diverse backgrounds to increase their understanding of what they are discussing with the teacher. McCarthey also found that students at all levels were able to develop a variety of interpretations of metaphors, leading them to deeply understand the concepts they were learning.

You can encourage your students to use metaphors in their writing, as McCarthey (1994) did. You can also use metaphors when conversing with students to enable them to think in a variety of different ways. In addition, you can create metaphors for students' situations, paraphrasing what they are saying. In the metaphors, of course, you want to help them visualize that they have been successful and that they have a happy and successful future.

• "Your situation is like you were in a swamp, and alligators were nipping at your heels. Suddenly, a helicopter comes and lifts you out of that. How does that feel?"

- "It sounds like it has been nighttime and dark for longer than you would have liked in your life, and you are emerging now into a beautiful, sunshiny day!"
- "In this class, you are in a garden filled with lovely growing things. You have only to decide which of them to pick first to put in your basket."
- "In this class, you are like a kid in a candy store. Many delicious things are available just for your choosing! You can have anything you want, and it is all free!"

Potential Functions for This Tip: Building Relationships, Teaching, Planning for the Future, Responding to Objections, Encouraging Students, Influencing Students, Resolving Conflicts

51. Models of the World

People have their own models of the world that they use to create their own reality. I go to Pilates class nearly every morning. A classmate came in one morning and said, "I rode my bicycle to the top of Bergen Mountain this morning before Pilates class." This would be totally inconsistent with my model of the world, as I don't ride a bicycle to the top of a mountain in the morning for fun. According to my model of the world, that would be sheer drudgery! Another woman jogs down a mountain to come to class, which amounts to approximately five miles per day, even during snowstorms. Still others would not be able to imagine attending Pilates classes on a regular basis, much less exercising.

Each learner has a different model of the world, as well. We can help students realize that their perceptions are just models of the world—not reality, not fact, and not truth. People create their models of the world by perceiving things differently. We can help students understand this concept by using phrases like the following:

- "Had you thought that you could talk with your neighbor during work time and still learn what you needed to learn in order to go to the next grade level?"

- "So in your model of the world, you had perceived that in that way."
- "Up until now, it has been your experience that you were able to pass courses without attending class. Since this class seems to be more difficult than other classes you have taken in the past, what are your thoughts as to what might help you do well in this class?"
- "Had you thought that the only way to learn was by reading a book?"
- "Had you thought that the only way to get the teacher's attention was to speak out of turn?"

Potential Functions for This Tip: Responding to Objections, Influencing Students, Resolving Conflicts

52. Naming Things Intentionally

The words that we use to name various times and activities during the day imply a variety of conditions and situations, setting the tone for the activity. Let's consider some of these phrases:

Passing time: What are some implications of these words? Students are passing between classes. What might be some alternative names? *Incubation time* suggests that students have an opportunity to think about what they have just been learning and incubate it in order to come up with even more new ideas. We could pose a question at the beginning of the *incubation time* for them to think about while they are walking to another location in the school. When they arrive, we could invite them to share their ideas and insights with a partner and then report to the whole group.

What are some implications of asking students to take a *break*? Students are pausing in their work. They are refreshing themselves. They are talking with their friends. We frequently talk about needing a *break*. The body tends to interpret what we tell it literally. Obviously, we want to avoid giving any messages to the body about having a *break,* as it may help us to do just that—break a leg, an arm, and so on. What are some alternative names? *Pause and refresh* might imply that they can refresh themselves for more learning. *Recharging batteries* could imply that they are gaining more energy for later.

When students go outside to play, we call it *recess*. What are some implications of this term? Students are taking a recess from their work in the classroom. They are going outside. What are some alternative names? *Playing with friends* puts the focus on the process of playing and friends. *Running and jumping* implies that they are moving actively. *Getting fresh air* implies that they are outside and refreshing themselves with new oxygen. *Incubating what we are learning* implies that students are learning even more as they are on the playground.

What are some implications of the term *homework*? Students are working at home. Many of us were raised having to do homework, which may not have been pleasant. The word "work" typically implies something difficult or unpleasant that has to be done before we can do other things that we enjoy. What are some other words to use instead of homework? How about *home play*? Other options include *extending your learning, making applications, applying your learning, expanding your learning,* and *playing with today's concepts*.

What other periods during the day might you choose to rename? Perhaps you could even invite the students to come up with new names and identify the presuppositions behind the various names.

Potential Functions for This Tip: Teaching, Influencing Students

53. Networking Students

According to Ladson-Billings (1994), "Culturally relevant teaching advocates the kind of cooperation that leads students to believe they cannot be successful without getting help from others or without being helpful to others" (p. 70). We can invite students to be "learning partners" with each other. Costa and Garmston (2002) discuss the importance of helping people to build interdependent relationships. We can also invite students to go to other students when they come to us with problems. Ladson-Billings suggests that when students feel supported by other students,

> The "school gang" becomes a viable alternative to the street gang. . . . Self-worth and self-concept is promoted in a very basic way, by acknowledging the individuals' worthiness to be a part of a supportive and loving group. (1994, p. 76)

Ask your students the following questions:

- "Who might you be able to help with what you are learning?"
- "With whom might you be able to share those insights?"
- "Who else might benefit from what you have studied so hard to learn?"
- "Who might you ask for assistance with that?"

Potential Functions for This Tip: Building Relationships, Teaching, Planning for the Future, Responding to Objections, Encouraging Students, Influencing Students, Resolving Conflicts

54. Next Steps

We would all love to have a crystal ball and know exactly where we are going, both in life and in the world—the next steps. At the least, we can help students to know the reasons behind what they are doing and to know the next steps that they will take in their learning.

My Pilates teacher sometimes explains, "You are doing this exercise to prepare you to do this new exercise," and she provides a demonstration of the new exercise. She is helping us to visualize the future and to see ourselves doing something that we would never dream that we could do! She will introduce an exercise and then show us three or four modifications that we will be doing soon "as our bodies are becoming even stronger." We watch in amazement. Then, several days or weeks later, we can do them, and she points that out. Follow her example with statements like the following:

- "As you become faster and faster on these drills in mathematics, you will soon be able to quickly and easily work complex math problems such as this." (Write a problem on the board that the students will be able to do soon and can't yet do.)
- "Today, we are doing this. Tomorrow, we are going to be building on what we did today in even more complex ways and doing problems such as this."
- "Let me show you the types of books that you will be reading in the next grade! Wow! The reason that we are reading these books today is to enable you to read those books next year . . . or even sooner than next year!"
- "Next year, you will be writing research papers. What we are doing today will help prepare you to write them."
- "Here is our schedule for the year. Each of you has a copy. As we move through the year, you can mark off the skills as you acquire them."

Potential Functions for This Tip: Teaching, Planning for the Future, Encouraging Students, Influencing Students, Resolving Conflicts

55. Not Tell You

It was mentioned earlier that the brain tends to delete words such as "no" and "not" (Hall, 2004). You can begin a phrase with the words "I'm not going to tell you" to help students internalize what comes after it. Students will hear, "I'm going to tell you," yet they will not be inclined to resist because we are not telling them anything. We can also emphasize the phrases that come afterward.

- "I'm *not going to tell you* that you should study. You should only study if you want to internalize the material so that you can use it in many contexts in the future."
- "I'm *not going to tell you* that this material will be helpful for you in many areas of your life. You can discover that for yourself."

- "I'm *not going to tell you* that you will be reaping many benefits from what you will be learning this year. You can discover that as you are making many applications."
- "I'm *not going to tell you* that this will be the best class you have ever taken. I'm going to let you find that out on your own."

Potential Functions for This Tip: Teaching, Responding to Objections, Influencing Students, Resolving Conflicts

56. "Noticed"

You can point out things that students are doing well and areas in which they are succeeding. You can say, "I noticed" or just say, "You did this or that"; however, because a general goal is to stay away from using the word "I" (see "Eliminating I" on p. 65), you can also say, "Noticed that you did this or that." It is important for us to be specific when we notice what students are doing well, rather than praising them in general terms (Meyer et al., 1979).

- "*Noticed* that you pushed your chair in when you got up."
- "*Noticed* that you helped your friend."
- "*Noticed* that you completed the assignment quickly."
- "*Noticed* that you turned in your homework on time."
- "*Noticed* from the smile on your face that you seemed to enjoy working on that project."

Potential Functions for This Tip: Building Relationships, Teaching, Responding to Objections, Encouraging Students, Influencing Students

57. One-Liners

When we feel stuck and discouraged, we tend to focus inward and don't want someone telling us what to do. We also don't want someone to make long, involved statements to us.

At times, students may feel stuck and discouraged. They may even indicate that they perceive that they can't do tasks, can't learn, or can't perform. Use one-liners to help them reorient their thinking and invite them to perceive differently (Hall, 2004).

- "How did you learn to perceive that in that way?"
- "How did you organize that perception in that way?"
- "What are you going to be doing when you have made that change?"
- "All the time?"
- "Tell me times when that was not the case."
- "Were you born thinking that?"

Potential Functions for This Tip: Responding to Objections, Encouraging Students, Influencing Students

58. Owning Successes

Have you ever done something well and had another person say, "I'm so proud of you"? While you probably didn't say anything at the time, you may have thought, "Why should *you* be proud? *I* am the one who should be proud!" Still, you accepted the comment.

Teachers might say, "I'm so proud of you!" "I really like that!" "I am happy about your accomplishments" or "I am pleased with what you did!" All of these statements, while well intended, imply to students that they are working to please the adult in their lives rather than themselves. Students generally want to please adults, and statements such as these suggest that their own feelings about their success don't matter. If they should happen to not be successful, they might be responsible for making the adult feel bad. Try using phrases like these when students are successful:

- "It must feel good to have succeeded!"
- "You must feel really great about what you did!"

- "The smile on your face suggests that you are really pleased with the progress that you are making!"
- "You really look happy about your successes."

Potential Functions for This Tip: Building Relationships, Teaching, Encouraging Students

59. Paraphrasing

We can show students that we are listening to them by paraphrasing what they say. This practice shows students that we understand what they are saying, or at least that we are trying to, according to Costa and Garmston (2002). Siu-Runyan (2001) suggests that when teachers invite students to talk about the stories they are going to write and truly listen to what they are saying, the students will be able to write more easily. How do we know that the person with whom we are talking is really listening to us? How many people actually listen to what we say and take the time to paraphrase us? We can give that gift to our students.

Ellison and colleagues (2008) suggest paraphrasing after a person finishes talking and before asking a question. They also discuss the importance of matching the emotions of people as well as the content of what they are saying. If someone is angry and talking in a loud voice, the person who is paraphrasing should also show anger and talk in a loud voice. If the person doing the paraphrasing were to talk in a soft voice, it would not match with the person who was angry, and the person might not feel "heard." Costa and Garmston (2007) identify three types of paraphrases: acknowledge and clarify, summarize and organize, and shift conceptual focus.

Acknowledge and Clarify

In the acknowledge and clarify paraphrase, you state back what the person says, acting like a mirror. Ellison and colleagues (2008) suggest avoiding using the word "I," as it puts the focus back on you, rather than on the other person. You may also want to avoid the phrase "what I think I hear you saying is . . . ," which was popular in the 1970s, as it tends to be overused and can come across as being less than sincere. Following are some examples of acknowledge and clarify paraphrases:

- "You are feeling sad today because your gerbil died."
- "You really feel good about the work you are doing in school."
- "You feel that you are making a difference with your project."

Summarize and Organize

Use the summarize and organize paraphrase to categorize what people say (Costa & Garmston, 2002). This technique puts thoughts into "containers," which can be a gift to students who think in random ways. I was recently talking with a student about possible ideas for her dissertation. She recognized that she had many ideas, yet she had no idea where to start. After listening to her, it appeared that she just had two main ideas. In my paraphrase, I said, "So you basically have two ideas: X and Y. All you need to do, then, is to decide which of them to do first." I wish I had had a camera! She exclaimed, "You're right! I do!" Following are some examples of summarize and organize paraphrases:

- "*First,* you plan to do X. *Then* you plan to do Y."
- "*On one hand,* you want to go outside and play, and *on the other hand,* you feel like you would really like to stay in and complete your work."
- "You have identified *three ideas* for your project and want to choose the one that will be the most fun for you to do. The *first idea* is X, the *second idea* is Y, and the *third idea* is Z."

Shift Conceptual Focus

When you shift conceptual focus for someone, you bring them to a higher or lower level of abstraction (Costa & Garmston, 2002). You help them see what is obvious to the observer, even though the person who is talking may not have quite been aware of it. You can invoke students' short- and long-range goals, higher purposes, identities, values, beliefs, concepts, or assumptions with the paraphrase. A paraphrase that shifts focus to a higher level of abstraction might look like these:

- "So a *goal* that you have is . . ."
- "So your *immediate goal* is X, and your *long-range goal* is Y."
- "So your *higher purpose or mission* for doing what you are doing is . . ."
- "So *you are* a peacemaker."
- "You *see yourself as* a successful person."
- "Something you *value* is . . ."
- "A *belief* that you strongly hold is . . ."
- "So what you are talking about is X (*concept*)."
- "An *assumption* that you hold is . . ."

A paraphrase that shifts focus to a lower level of abstraction might look like these:

- "So you are *not* talking about Y."
- "*An example* of what you are talking about would be Z."

Potential Functions for This Tip: Building Relationships, Teaching, Planning for the Future, Responding to Objections, Encouraging Students, Influencing Students, Resolving Conflicts

60. Past Tense

We all have problems, deal with them, get over them, and move on. We can use language to assist students in realizing that they, too, can resolve their problems and move on with their lives.

When students state problems in present tense, they are implying that they believe that they have always had a problem, continue to have a problem, and will always have the problem (Andreas, 1992). No possibility exists for change. They might say the following:

- "I *have* this problem."
- "I *can't* do X."
- "I *am* like this."
- "I *am always* angry."

We can use the words "have" and "used to" to help students to place the limitation that they think they have in the past. We might reply in the following ways:

- "So you *have had* that problem."
- "You *used to* think you couldn't do X."
- "In the past, you *have perceived* that you were like that. What happens as you are changing the way you thought about it?"
- "So you *used to* be angry."

We can also use "had," saying, "You had done X." That puts the action even farther in the past:

- "You *had had* that problem."
- "You *had thought* that you couldn't do X."
- "You *had had* a perception that you were like that."
- "You *had felt* angry."

Potential Functions for This Tip: Teaching, Responding to Objections, Encouraging Students, Influencing Students, Resolving Conflicts

61. Perceiving

We all have different ways of arriving at conclusions that become reality for us. One person's reality is not necessarily the truth, nor is it necessarily another person's reality. During the 2006 holiday season, the Denver area received several large snowstorms, each totaling approximately two to three feet. Denver International Airport was closed several times, and people had widely varying perceptions about the situation. Some people welcomed the snow and went out for walks, played in the snow, and had fun. People who spent the night at the airport on their way to see loved ones were less than pleased. Some motorists felt angry because they felt that the snowplows didn't clean the roads quickly enough. Each person had a different perception of the situation, resulting in widely varying attitudes about the snowstorms. Each person created his or her reality, resulting in various emotions, including anger, disgust, happiness, excitement, and so on.

When learners make statements that appear to be reality for them, yet can potentially be harmful for their learning in the long run, invite them to share how they arrived at that perception or view. You can use words such as "think," "feel," "interpret," "label," "categorize," and "seem" in place of "perceive." You can help learners to see that since what they thought was "truth" is actually only a "perception," they can change their perceptions by deciding to perceive things differently.

We create our reality by the way we perceive things and by what we tell ourselves about what we perceive. When people perceive things as being problems, they are often looking at them through one specific model of the world (Hall, 2006). People tend to base decisions on what they believe to be the only correct way of viewing things. When you imply that students are responsible for their own perceptions, you open them up to the possibility of choosing other perceptions.

- "What had you *told yourself* about it that led you to *interpret* her behavior in that way?"
- "So for you, *at this point in time,* you had *labeled* it as a problem."
- "What had you *perceived* in that situation *up until now*?"
- "How did you arrive at that *perception*?"
- "What were some of your *perceptions* that led you to *formulate that view* of things?"
- "How did you know how to *define* this as a problem?"

Potential Functions for This Tip: Responding to Objections, Influencing Students, Resolving Conflicts

62. Planning

Students may be totally motivated to do a task and have no idea how to go about doing it. Thus, when they don't complete their assignments, they may not intend to be obstinate. They just don't know how to go about accomplishing the tasks.

Years ago, I learned to break large tasks down into doable segments that could be accomplished rapidly. My parents made their yearly visit to see my husband and me in Colorado. Usually, when people came to visit, I would clear out the closet in the room they were going to stay in and throw things under the bed in another bedroom. As you can imagine, my house was not exactly neat.

My father let me know that my house was a mess, and I needed to clean it. Needless to say, I was devastated. I got out a pencil and paper and started writing a list of things to do. I perceived that "clean the front bedroom" was too large a task, so I broke the task down into smaller bits, such as "clean the closet in the front bedroom," "clean under the bed in the front bedroom," and so on, addressing each room in the house. When I finished the list, I had 45 tasks to do. Since I was teaching at the elementary level and it was summertime, I decided to do one task per day. After doing each task, I would go out and jog or do something else that was fun for me. Without knowing it, I was taking "joy breaks," which McGee-Cooper (1992, 1993) recommends.

The answer to the question, "How do you eat an elephant?" is, of course, "One bite at a time." After you have determined which bites to take, it is helpful to jot down approximately how long each task will take. If a task will take quite a long time to do, you can write down how long you are willing to spend each day on that task. As a result, even if you have a long list of tasks, if they are only 10 minutes long, you will feel a sense of being able to accomplish what you want to. If some of the tasks are long and others are short, you can intersperse the short tasks with the longer ones, depending on your energy level.

The final step in planning is to determine the approximate order in which you will eat the different bites of the elephant. What do you have the most energy for? Which step will open up the other steps? Perhaps you will do all of the short tasks first to get them over with, or perhaps you will focus on one step until you have completed it. It is helpful to see yourself moving quickly and easily through each of the tasks and feeling excited along the way about how rapidly you are progressing toward the goal!

McGee-Cooper (1993) has numerous suggestions for making planning fun and enjoyable. When I was doing an internship with her in the summer of 1990, I commented on the attractiveness of the red planner in which she kept her "To Do" lists. She said that the color red gave her energy. Since then, I have had a red planner. She also suggested numerous right-brained organizational strategies, such as using sticky notes and colored markers, accomplishing several tasks at once, knowing what to spend a lot of time doing and what to spend less time doing, and other strategies for making planning fun!

Potential Functions for This Tip: Teaching, Planning for the Future, Encouraging Students, Resolving Conflicts

63. Pointing Out Growth

We all want others to notice what we are learning, how we are changing, and what we are accomplishing. My Pilates instructor frequently comments on the class's growth. She mentions where we were a few weeks ago and what we are able to do now, with comments like these:

- "Do you remember a couple of weeks ago when you weren't able to do this exercise? Now you are doing it easily!"
- "See how much stronger you are getting? Do you remember when you perceived this exercise to be difficult?"

Ginsberg and Wlodkowski (2000) discuss the importance of students feeling competent at what they are learning. According to

Ginsberg (2004), teachers can use techniques "that help students authentically identify what they know and can do and that give students a sense of hope" (p. 12). She includes strategies such as using rubrics, inviting students to assess themselves, and helping students demonstrate what they know in contexts that are relevant to them. Consider the following statements:

- "As you remember back to 1st grade and the types of books that you were reading, did you ever imagine that you would be reading books that were this thick?"
- "You may remember back to the time when you were first learning what a globe was. Now you are locating countries all over the globe!"
- "Think back to the beginning of the school year, when you only knew how to print. Now you are writing in cursive and getting even better every day!"

Potential Functions for This Tip: Teaching, Responding to Objections, Encouraging Students, Influencing Students

64. Points of View

Have you ever been in a large stadium? What was the view like when you went into it? What was the view like when you went to one end of it, looking back? If you were able to climb up into the higher levels, how did that enable you to gain other perspectives on the stadium? If you were to fly over the stadium in an airplane, you would see it from yet another perspective.

Typically, when people are feeling stuck, it is because they are viewing the situation from only one perspective. We can help students see things from different points of view (Dilts & DeLozier, 2000). We can invite students to step in and become another person, seeing out of that person's eyes, hearing out of that person's ears, thinking that person's thoughts, and feeling that person's feelings. Students can also observe a situation from the point of view of a neutral observer who is an equal distance from them and the other person. Another possibility could be to suggest that the student go to a "balcony," a place above the two people, to get a different view. Statements that could help students to see a situation from the point of view of another person include the following:

- "If you were your mother, what might you say about the work?"
- "Pretend that you are your friend. What might you be thinking right now? What might you want to say?"
- "For just a moment, become your friend, looking out of his or her eyes and feeling what he or she might be feeling right now. What are some of your insights as to what your friend might want from you right now?"

Following are some statements to help students take the point of view of a neutral observer:

- "As you stand an equal distance between you and your friend, what are some of the things that you notice as the two people interact?"
- "Taking the position of a neutral observer, what might be some new insights that you can gather?"

We can also invite students to go to the balcony, seeing both themselves and the other person from above:

- "If you were to go to a balcony and observe the conversation between you and your friend, what might be some advice that you would offer to your friend, and what might be some advice that you would offer to yourself?"
- "From the balcony position, what might be some of the things that you notice as the two people interact?"

Potential Functions for This Tip: Teaching, Planning for the Future, Responding to Objections, Encouraging Students, Resolving Conflicts

65. Positive Words

We can encourage or discourage students, invite them or disinvite them, depending on the words that we use. How do the following words make you feel?

- bad
- difficult
- hard
- failure
- limitations
- neglected
- no
- overwhelmed
- problem
- wrong

In contrast, how do these words make you feel?

- curiosity
- discovery
- effective
- exploring
- happiness
- joyful
- moving forward
- possibilities
- potential
- opportunities
- options
- resources

By choosing the words that you use with students with care and thought, you can help encourage them to learn. You can also discuss the impact of the words that students choose on their feelings and the feelings of others.

Potential Functions for This Tip: Building Relationships, Teaching, Planning for the Future, Responding to Objections, Encouraging Students, Influencing Students, Resolving Conflicts

66. Pretending as Though You Can

Do you remember playing the child's game "Pretend"? Invite learners to use their imaginations to pretend that they can do certain things that they may not yet be able to do.

If students say that they can't do something or that they don't know how to do something, you first need to make sure that you have thoroughly explained how to do the task and answered all of their questions. If you sense that their hesitation is not because of a lack of instruction but because they are reluctant to try something new, suggest that they pretend as though they can do it. By having them create a vision in their minds of themselves succeeding beyond their wildest dreams, you can assist them in moving forward in ways that they had not yet been able to imagine. If a student says, "I can't do this," possible responses include the following:

- "What if you could? What might that be like?"
- "Act as though you could. What might you be doing?"
- "If you could, what might be some of your first steps?"
- "What might you be doing if you were able to do it?"
- "If you could do it, what might it look like? What would you be seeing, hearing, and feeling?"
- "Just pretend that you can. What are you doing in order to complete it?"

Potential Functions for This Tip: Teaching, Planning for the Future, Responding to Objections, Encouraging Students, Influencing Students, Resolving Conflicts

67. Questions from Students

We have all had times when we declined to ask a question, even though we had one, because of the way someone asked us if we had any questions. It could have been the person's tone of voice, or it could have been the way that the person phrased the question.

The way we ask for student questions can be either inviting or disinviting. Obviously, we want to ask for their questions in such a way as to invite them to ask and help them to feel comfortable. We want them to know that their questions are both wanted and valued.

Grinder (personal communication, September 1995) suggested stepping to a new place, away from the spot where you present information, when you invite students to ask questions. Thus, you show students that when you are in this particular spot, they can ask questions. You also should use an approachable voice, bobbing your head up and down and curling your voice up at the end of the question. Your palms can also be turned up.

These are some inviting ways of asking questions:

• "What might be some of the questions that you have about the material that we just covered?"

• "As you consider the material that we are discussing, what are some of the areas that are not yet clear?"

• "What questions might you have about the applications of the material that we are learning?"

These are some disinviting ways to ask for questions:

• "Who has a question?"
• "Any questions?"
• "Does anyone have a question?"

Potential Functions for This Tip: Building Relationships, Teaching, Resolving Conflicts

68. Questions That Invite

Every day on the news, we hear questions. "Will the trend continue?" "Is he guilty?" "What will happen next? Stay tuned. We will have the answers for you tomorrow." We cannot avoid processing the question, whether we answer it or not. We are compelled to internalize the question and attempt to answer it.

Recently, a friend asked me, "What do you most love in what you are doing?" According to Hall (2004), "every question sets a direction and directs the listener how to think" (p. 47). Through our questions, we access students' experiences and resources. In addition, we build or deepen rapport with them and invite them to process information in new and different ways.

Some possible goals in asking questions of students could be to find out what they already know, what they would like to know, and what they don't yet fully understand. We can also ask questions to help them to be more precise in their language, and we can ask questions to help them to expand their thinking (Costa & Garmston, 2007).

Costa and Garmston (2007) identify seven strategies for asking invitational questions to mediate the thinking of others. The strategies include using an approachable voice, using plurals, using tentative language, using positive presuppositions, asking open-ended questions, inviting the person to use cognitive operations, and focusing on content that is either internal to the person or outside of the person.

Using an Approachable Voice

Grinder (2007) identifies two kinds of voices. One is the approachable voice, in which the head goes up and down while the person is talking, causing the voice to go up and down. The palms of the hands are generally face-up when we use an approachable voice, as when we are asking for something. When we talk with young children, we tend to use this type of voice frequently in order to build rapport and show that we are approachable. Women tend to use this type of voice more than men.

Grinder also defines the credible voice. When a person uses this voice, the head remains still while he or she talks. At the end of sentences, the head tends to go down. The palms of the hands generally face down when people are talking in a credible voice. They are sending information. Thus, they come across as knowing what they are talking about.

Grinder suggests that we use the approachable voice when we ask questions. We can move our head up and down (not too much, depending on the grade level and depending on our gender—less for men than for women). By having our palms up, we convey that we are asking for an answer.

Using Plurals

Costa and Garmston (2007) also suggest that we use plurals when asking questions. By doing so, we communicate with students that many answers could be correct, and that no one right answer exists. What is your response to being asked, "What is your goal?" You may start searching for a goal. The presupposition behind that question is that you only have one goal. What is your response to being asked, "What are your goals?" This question presupposes that not only do you have a goal but that you have more than one. More than one right answer exists, and whatever answer you give will be fine. Physiologically, the question enables the brain to feel comfortable enough to think of multiple goals.

Using Tentative Language

Costa and Garmston (2007) also suggest using tentative language when asking questions. Words such as "might," "could be," "possibilities," "possible," and "hunches" can serve to further relax the person, opening up numerous possibilities for responding. By using tentative language combined with plurals, we let the person know that many answers could be possible, and any response will be just fine.

- "What *might be* some of your goals?"
- "What *could be* some of your goals?"
- "What *might* be some *possible* goals for yourself?"
- "What are your *hunches* about what goals you will achieve?"
- "What are some goal *possibilities*?"

Consider the differences between the following questions:

- "What is your *idea*?" (singular)
- "What are your *ideas*?" (plural)
- "What *might be some* of your *ideas*?" (plural and tentative language)

Using Positive Presuppositions

Presuppositions are facts embedded in the questions we ask. Every question contains presuppositions. Ladson-Billings (1994) reports that Elizabeth Harris begins her 2nd grade class every day by asking her students, "What are we going to be our best at today?" (p. 48). The presuppositions behind her question were that all of the students in her class were going to be their best at something that day, and it was only a matter of deciding what it would be. When the day is over,

> each student is given an opportunity to describe what she or he did to be successful during the day. Students report on successes and reflect on ways they could have been even better at some things. Harris constantly tells them how good they are. (p. 48)

What are the presuppositions in the following questions?

- "How long have you been working on this?" (that the person is working on a project and has been working on it for a period of time)
- "When are you going to start working?" (that the person is not working and is, hopefully, going to start working soon)

You can consciously embed many positive presuppositions into your questions to imply that the person you are talking to is intelligent and thoughtful. Positive presuppositions, along with plurals and tentative language, might look like this:

- "What are your hunches as to what might be some of the goals that will help you advance toward your future in ways that are exciting and fun for you?"
- "What might be some of the ideas that you have been thinking of that will help you and your team finish the project in a creative and enjoyable way in record time?"
- "As someone who seeks to do a good job, what have been some of your thoughts about how you might go about doing this project?"
- "As you consider what you are going to do for this assignment, what might be some possible ways to begin?"
- "Based on your knowledge of the topic, what could be some areas that you would like to consider as you are developing the project?"
- "As a highly trained professional, what might be some of your impressions of the material you are learning?"
- "As someone who thinks deeply about various things, what might be some of the connections that you are making?"

Asking Open-Ended Questions

Costa and Garmston (2007) recommend asking questions that are open-ended so that many answers could be possible. They suggest starting questions with "an interrogative, not a verb," such as "'*What* is your thinking about . . .?' versus '*Have* you thought about . . . .?'" (p. 44).

Using Words That Imply Cognitive Operations

You can also use words that invite people to think in specific ways. Costa and Garmston (2007) suggest the following:

- Input: recall, define, describe, identify, name, list

• Process: compare, infer, analyze, sequence, synthesize, summarize

• Output: predict, evaluate, speculate, imagine, envision, hypothesize (p. 45)

Rather than saying, "Tell me about the story," you could say, "Please *describe* the sequence of events in the story." Rather than "Please tell me some possible endings for the story," you could say, "What might be some of your *predictions* for how the story might end?"

Addressing Internal and External Content

According to Costa and Garmston (2007), we can invite students to think about content that is internal to them, as well as content that is external. They identify five states of mind that are beneficial for educators to have: consciousness, craftsmanship, efficacy, flexibility, and interdependence. Examples of questions that help students to focus on internal content include the following:

• "As you were completing the assignment quickly, what were some of the feelings that you noticed?" (consciousness)

• "What were some of the strategies and processes that you used to achieve your goals?" (craftsmanship)

• "What are some of the many times that you have been successful in doing this in the past?" (efficacy)

• "What might be some of the various strategies that you could use to accomplish this?" (flexibility)

• "Who might be some of the people on whom you could call for assistance as you launch into this new project?" (interdependence)

We can also ask students questions about external content:

• "What might be some of the resources that you could access as you complete the project in this unit?"

• "How might you compare and contrast the character qualities of the two main characters in the story?"

Types of Questions to Avoid

Costa and Kallik (2008) suggest avoiding asking the following types of questions:

- *Verification questions,* in which the teacher and student both already know the answer: "What is the capital of the United States?"
- *Closed questions,* in which students can answer "yes" or "no": "Can you tell me X?"
- *Rhetorical questions,* in which the question contains the answer to the question: "How many hours does a five-hour work shift last?"
- *Defensive questions,* in which students may need to defend their actions: "Why don't you know the answer?"
- *Agreement questions,* in which the teacher is asking the student to agree: "You agree with me, don't you?"

Potential Functions for This Tip: Building Relationships, Teaching, Planning for the Future, Responding to Objections, Encouraging Students, Influencing Students, Resolving Conflicts

69. Refining Versus Improving

What do we imply when we ask a student to improve his or her paper? We are suggesting that the paper is not good. On the other hand, what do we imply when we ask the student to *refine* the paper? We are suggesting that the paper is already good and could be *even better!*

Use the word "refine" instead of "improve" when talking with students about their work. By doing so, you suggest that the paper is already fine. Even if it isn't, you want to make the student feel strong so that he or she is more capable of making the changes you suggest.

- "Please *refine* the paper."
- "Could you please *refine* the project based on these suggestions?"

- "I'm wondering what might be some of your ideas and suggestions for *refining* the paper."

Potential Functions for This Tip: Building Relationships, Teaching, Encouraging Students,

70. Reframing

Have you ever felt stuck about doing something and, as soon as you changed the way you were looking at it, you were able to accomplish it? Learners who state objections may be focusing on something small or something quite large. Either way, we can help them to see things differently by changing the size of the frame that they are putting around their problem. If they have a small frame, we can help them to put a large frame around the picture. If they have a large frame around the picture, we can help them use a small frame. This is called "reframing" (Bandler & Grinder, 1982).

Pictures look different depending on which frame we put around them, be they oil paintings, photographs, or posters. The children's book *Zoom* (Banyai, 1998) is a great example of reframing. The photographer begins with a close-up of part of a rooster's comb. In each succeeding picture, he moves out farther, including more in the picture and putting a larger frame around the picture. The picture at the end of the book is of the Earth from far away.

Here are some examples of reframing student objections by moving from a close-in shot to a larger frame:

- "I don't see how I will ever be able to use this."
- ○ "As you go out 5, 10, perhaps 15 years into the future, imagining your future starting now and seeing yourself in many different contexts of your life, what might be some of the areas that you notice in which you are applying all that you are learning?"
- "I don't have enough time today to do this assignment because I have an appointment after school."
- ○ "Looking at the week as a whole, when might you be able to set aside some time to do it?"

At other times, students may be seeing too large a chunk and need to see smaller chunks in order to feel confident in accomplishing a task. Have you ever felt that a task was too overwhelming to tackle? Just the thought of trying to do it sends us scurrying to find something else to do.

Students may feel a sense of being overwhelmed when they get ready to write a dissertation or begin a large project. One doctoral student said that her dissertation looked like a large mountain that she would never be able to climb. This way of perceiving the dissertation resulted in her feeling a sense of paralysis, which in turn created fear and dread. As a result, she found everything else to do except begin writing the dissertation. I was able to help her place frames around the smaller pieces by inviting her to mentally blast the mountain and then pick up one stone at a time from the rubble.

A strategy that I have often used with students who are writing a larger paper is to have them brainstorm the various sections that they will include. Then they key these into the computer, with page breaks between the topics. I joke with them that the dissertation is basically done—all they have to do is fill in the blanks! They might work on one section one day and another section on another day. Before they know it, they are finished.

Some examples of reframing student objections from larger to smaller follow:

- "It looks like a mountain! I will never be able to do it!"
- "What are some of the pieces that you will be breaking it into as you are completing it?"
- "That is a large task. It really feels overwhelming!"
- "Let's brainstorm some of the smaller tasks that you will be doing as you are working on it."

Potential Functions for This Tip: Teaching, Planning for the Future, Responding to Objections, Encouraging Students, Influencing Students, Resolving Conflicts

71. Resources

Have you ever felt that you were not able to do a task, but that if you only had more resources, you would be able to do it? Still, you were not sure which resources to access or where to get them.

When students are feeling "stuck," they generally feel like they are lacking in resources. We can help them to notice the resources that have been available all along. What external and internal resources are available to them that they had not recognized until now? You can point out specific resources to students, or you can invite them to explore the many resources that are available by asking them questions such as the following:

• "I'm wondering what resources that you haven't accessed yet will assist you in the process of completing this project."

• "As you look around the room, noticing your colleagues who are incredible resources, who might you be able to call on first?"

• "What internal and external resources might you access that will enable you to complete the project quickly and joyfully?"

• "As you think of the tremendous wealth of resources in the library, which databases might you be able to access first?"

• "I wonder if you have recognized yet all of the resources that are inside of you that you have used in the past for succeeding in other situations."

• "Are you curious now to recognize the many resources that are available to you as you are in the process of moving forward toward achieving your exciting goals?"

• "Have you yet noticed your enriching capabilities that have been there all along and can assist you in the process of achieving your goals?"

Potential Functions for This Tip: Teaching, Planning for the Future, Responding to Objections, Encouraging Students, Influencing Students, Resolving Conflicts

72. Review, Review, Review

An old joke: A young man in New York City stops someone on the street, asking, "How do you get to Carnegie Hall?" Thinking that the young man wants to play at the esteemed musical venue, the New Yorker responds, "Practice, practice, practice."

How do we assist our students in learning? Review, review, review. How many times have we thought, "I said this, yet they didn't learn it! They must not have been listening. They should know it because I said it one time." In reality, even when we attend classes as adults, do we necessarily listen to every word that the presenter says? Do our minds ever wander in learning situations? Of course they do, as do the minds of our students! When teachers repeat concepts, reviewing them for us, they are helping us to learn even more deeply. How do we get our students to learn? Review, review, review!

Potential Functions for This Tip: Teaching, Resolving Conflicts

73. "Say More About That"

What happens when people phrase questions as statements in a gentle and inquiring voice? "Please say more about that." "Help me understand your reasoning behind doing that." "Talk about your thoughts in relation to X." These types of questions tend to be gentle, eliciting thoughtful answers.

- "Please elaborate."
- "Tell us more."
- "Please continue."
- "Please talk more about your perceptions."

Potential Functions for This Tip: Teaching, Planning for the Future, Responding to Objections, Resolving Conflicts

74. Self-Assessing

Do you remember when you were in school and you received your graded papers back from the teacher? What did you do with them? Did you take them home and treasure them, or were you more inclined to put them in the nearest trash can unless you needed to make corrections on them? All of the hard work that the teacher had done was lost. Have you ever watched your students place the papers that you so carefully graded in the trash can the first chance they got, or did you ever pick up students' papers off the ground by the bus stop?

As teachers, we tend to spend much of our time judging student work. Why should we have all of the fun? When students assess their work, it not only helps us out but also teaches them to take another point of view. Use statements like the following to have students assess their own or each other's papers:

• "Circle three examples that you like, and place a check mark by three examples that you might do differently the next time."

• "Write three sentences stating things that you like about the work. Write three sentences stating things that you would like to improve the next time."

• "Fill out the rubric, checking one through four for each of the criteria for the assignment."

• "Place a happy face by the three items that were your favorites, and underline the three items that you might like to change."

• "Exchange papers with the person next to you. Please use the rubric to assess the paper."

• "Talk with the person sitting next to you about what you liked about your paper and what you might do differently the next time."

Potential Functions for This Tip: Teaching, Resolving Conflicts

75. "Someone Said . . ."

Has anyone ever told you about what someone else said that had implications for you? When I was growing up, my parents often told me things that other people said that were really directed toward me: "Mary was telling me yesterday that her daughter was enjoying being in 5th grade and was working really hard." The underlying message was that I should enjoy being in 5th grade and work really hard, too. Recently, I was pondering taking a few days' leave from my job. A friend said, "Let me read a letter to you that my mother sent to me: 'Dear Jane, I know that you believe that you are indispensable to everyone. Let me assure you that others can step in during your absence and do just as good a job!'" Point made—I took the leave!

When you don't want to say something directly to a student, you can talk about what someone told you, what your parents told you, what the principal told you, what you heard on television, and so on. The student isn't able to reject it as advice coming from you, as it is not your advice. It is just something that someone told you.

- "A friend of mine told me that his learning experiences brought him many new insights and understandings, leading to even greater possibilities in his life."
- "One of my students from last year said that his year in this class made profound changes in his life by helping him to know that he could truly learn anything that he wanted to learn. He also said that by applying his new learnings, his life changed in many different and exciting ways."
- "According to your teacher from last year, you are an exciting group of students with huge potential."

You can also quote research studies and experts to drive home points that you wish to make. I worked with Michael Grinder on a three-year training program in my school district. He trained "Green Chair" coaches to coach teachers in their schools in classroom management. Instead of having the coaches tell the teachers what to do, he suggested that the coaches say, "Michael says . . ." in order to put the blame on Michael. The coaches weren't telling the teachers what to do; they were just saying what Michael said.

- "According to (author), students who set future goals to achieve are more successful than students who focus only on today."
- "(Author) found that when students can see their lives along a continuum and visualize themselves 1 year, 5 years, 10 years, 20 years, 50 years, and so on in the future, they move toward realizing their dreams more quickly than students who only look at today."

Potential Functions for This Tip: Building Relationships, Teaching, Planning for the Future, Responding to Objections, Encouraging Students, Influencing Students, Resolving Conflicts

76. Specifying

We all make statements such as, "Nobody is doing this," "Everybody is going," "You always do that," and so on. Of course we know that in reality, some people are doing that, not everybody in the entire world is going, and there are times when you don't do that.

When I taught 7th grade, I was telling a colleague that the students in one of my classes were not behaving well. She asked, "Which students, specifically?" When I thought about it, I realized that only two students needed to change their behavior.

We can help others to clarify what they are saying and to realize that "everybody" may be only one person. If one of your colleagues says, "The students are out of control," ask, "Which students, specifically?" If one of your students says, "Nobody likes me," respond, "Nobody? Not one person? Who might be some people who like you?"

Costa and Garmston (2007) suggest that by asking these probing questions, we are helping students to become more precise in their thinking. Here are student comments and some possible responses:

- "Nobody likes me."
- ○ "You don't have even one friend?"
- "Everyone is mean to me."
- ○ "Everyone? Not even one person is kind to you?"
- "He always does that."
- ○ "Always? He's not doing it now, is he?"

You can also model eliminating these generalizations from your vocabulary for students. By being specific when you talk, you can teach students to be specific when they talk. Here are some phrases to omit, followed by statements to put in their place.

- "You always do that."
- ○ "Yesterday, this situation occurred on the playground in which you were involved."
- "You never come in from recess on time."
- ○ "Today and last Friday, you came in from recess three minutes after the bell had rung."

Potential Functions for This Tip: Building Relationships, Teaching, Planning for the Future, Responding to Objections, Encouraging Students, Influencing Students, Resolving Conflicts

77. "Stop And . . ."

Stop and think about just how powerful an impact you are having on the lives of many students, as well as those with whom they come into contact, both now and for many years to come. Stop and reflect on the joy that you are gaining and spreading to all around you.

What do we do when we hear the word "stop"? We stop, of course! We can invite learners to stop for just a moment and consider something new. We can get them to stop their behavior and listen to us.

- "*Stop just a moment and* think about the possible outcomes from this action."

- "*Stop and* listen to the instructions right now so that you will know what to do."
- "*Stop and* notice the many new ideas and insights that you are gaining as a result of focusing on the class and thinking about your new discoveries."
- "*Stop and* visualize the many avenues already opening up to you and for you as you move along the pathway toward even greater potential."
- "*Stop and* get a sense of all of the new learnings that you have acquired through persevering in this class."

Potential Functions for This Tip: Teaching, Responding to Objections, Encouraging Students, Influencing Students, Resolving Conflicts

78. Strengths

When I taught seminars on "Discipline with Love and Logic" for Jim Fay and Foster Cline in the 1980s, they had an overhead transparency that facilitators were to use that said, "It is only possible to build from strengths." How true! I have thought about that quote numerous times over the years. When students feel strong, they can succeed. Truly, it is perhaps *only* when students are feeling strong that they can succeed at the highest levels. What might we be able to do to help students know their strengths and build on them? Pauline Dupree, a teacher in Ladson-Billings's (1994) study, was "always on the lookout for ways to recognize and affirm student accomplishments" (pp. 98–99). In addition, she recognized and affirmed both the strengths that students showed in class and their strengths outside of class. According to Ladson-Billings,

> Dupree's in-class recognition of out-of-class excellence encourages the students to conceive of excellence broadly. It also begins to create a stronger connection between home and school. Once students see that Dupree makes a fuss about the things they enjoy, they seek similar recognition in the classroom. (p. 99)

As a closure activity for a seminar I attended, the instructor asked each participant to tape a piece of paper to our backs. Then we wrote affirming comments, comments of appreciation, and comments acknowledging each other's strengths on each other's backs. When we removed the pieces of paper from our backs at the end of the activity, many people had tears in their eyes. I would imagine that participants will keep the piece of paper throughout their lives. Invite class members to write each student's strengths on a piece of paper in a similar activity.

Peggy Valentine, a teacher in Ladson-Billings's (1994) study, asked students to nominate other students for "excellence awards." Students were affirmed and their strengths were acknowledged by other students, rather than just by the teacher. In addition to creating an atmosphere and leading activities in which students affirm each other's strengths, possible ways to affirm, acknowledge, and build on students' strengths include statements such as these:

• "Wow! You are truly a writer!" (mathematician, artist, scientist, etc.)
• "You consistently make 100 percent on your mathematics assignments."
• "A real strength for you is _____!"
• "You are really good at writing!" (doing mathematics, drawing, singing, etc.)

Potential Functions for This Tip: Building Relationships, Teaching, Planning for the Future, Responding to Objections, Encouraging Students, Influencing Students, Resolving Conflicts

79. Student Names

We all like to hear our names. By using students' names, we are affirming and honoring them: "Yes, Melinda, you are correct." "Tom, you worked hard on your project." "Yes, María, the papers are due tomorrow." Prusak and colleagues (2005) recommend that teachers use each student's name during a class period. They also emphasize the importance of using students' names for positive reinforcement, rather than for negative feedback.

Often, students have special names that they prefer to be called. By asking students what name they would like to be called, you model respect for them and help to build a positive relationship with them. The name that is listed on the student roster at the beginning of the year is not necessarily what students would like to be called.

If you teach many classes, the need for knowing and using student names is even greater. Physical education teachers, music teachers, and art teachers who see every student in the school need to use student names just as much as classroom teachers need to use them. Teachers at higher levels who see a different group of students each day also need to learn names quickly.

What are some strategies that you can use to learn students' names? First, you need to believe that knowing students' names is important and value the students themselves. Below are some strategies that can help.

• Invite students to get to know each others' names along with you. Have students sit in a circle and each give their name and something they would like members of the class to know about them. Then, classmates could name each student in the room, going around the circle.

• As you meet each student, write the student's name on your hand with a finger, say the student's name to yourself, and picture the student's name emblazoned on his or her forehead in an interesting manner (in denim if the student is wearing jeans, in red if the student is wearing red, etc.).

• Make a seating chart with the students' names and where they sit. Spend time at the beginning of school memorizing the students' names.

Potential Functions for This Tip: Building Relationships, Teaching, Planning for the Future, Responding to Objections, Encouraging Students, Influencing Students, Resolving Conflicts

80. Systems Approach

Flicker and Hoffman (2006) suggest that educators would benefit from using a systems approach to examine the many possible reasons that students tend to misbehave in the classroom and formulate interventions accordingly. In the same manner, we can use a systems approach to help students accomplish what they want to accomplish. Ask yourself the following questions:

• "Does the student have a higher purpose for doing this that will result in him or her moving toward the goal more quickly?" When students are working toward a degree for higher purposes, everyone had better get out of the way! I have also found that when students seem to be less motivated, they tend to not be thinking of their higher purpose for completing their degrees. By reminding them of their higher purposes, we can help them move toward accomplishing their goals even more quickly. Students at all ages can have higher purposes for learning what they are learning.

• "Does the student have a relationship with me?" For whom are students going to work harder—someone they dislike, or someone they like?

• "Does the student have the skills to do what he or she would like to accomplish?" We tend to do things that we feel competent at doing; on the other hand, we tend to put off doing things that we don't believe that we have the skills to do. Students who are not good readers (or have the identity that they are poor readers) tend to do things other than read.

• "Does the student believe that he or she has the skills to accomplish what he or she would like to accomplish?" One part of moving forward and succeeding is having the skills to accomplish what we want to do, and another part is *believing* that we have the skills. Point out instances to students in which they demonstrated the skills in question. If we tell students that they are good writers and they don't believe us, they may tend to write poorly just to prove that they are poor writers. On the other hand, when we can point to evidence that students have the skills, they will be more likely to believe us: "I only made five edits in the work that you turned in yesterday." "You lined up to come in from recess on time every day the last month." Gradually, by showing students evidence, we will help them to believe in their abilities and competencies.

• "Is the student willing to work hard and focus on the project in order to accomplish it?" Students need to be able to commit to doing work in order to complete the project.

• "Can the student examine the project and break it into doable pieces in order to complete it?" We have discussed the importance of students deciding on the parts of the task, the length of time to spend on each task, and the sequence in which to do the tasks.

• "How can I help the student to associate areas in which he has succeeded with other areas that he would like to learn?" Ask students to talk about things that they do well, including goals for doing those things, strategies used, strategies to use when the other strategies do not work, and outcomes of working toward the goals. Then ask students to "pretend as if" they were using these goals and strategies with the area that they would like to learn.

Potential Functions for This Tip: Building Relationships, Teaching, Planning for the Future, Responding to Objections, Encouraging Students, Influencing Students, Resolving Conflicts

81. Tag Questions

Have you ever heard someone make a statement and follow it by asking, "Don't you agree?" "Haven't they?" "Hasn't it?" These are called "tag questions" (Andreas, 1992, p. 52). We generally say, "Yes," whether we had previously agreed with the statement or not.

You can add tag questions at the end of statements to emphasize your point and get students to agree with you. When they say, "yes," they will be more willing to accept what you just said, and they will believe it even more deeply. Of course, you need to say things with which they can agree.

- "You have really been studying hard, *haven't you?*"
- "You really understand this material, *don't you?*"
- "We are having a great day, *aren't we?*"
- "That used to be a problem, *didn't it?*"
- "You are really wanting to learn this, *aren't you?*"

Potential Functions for This Tip: Building Relationships, Teaching, Planning for the Future, Responding to Objections, Encouraging Students, Influencing Students, Resolving Conflicts

82. "That" Versus "This"

What do you perceive when someone says, "I want this"? Where is "this" located in your field of vision? What do you perceive when someone says, "I want that"? Where is "that" located in your field of vision? Most people will perceive something as being closer to them when they hear the word "this" and farther away from them when they hear the word "that."

You can use the word "that" to put something farther away from the person with whom you are talking, and you can use the word "this" to move it closer to the person. It all depends on your purpose in the conversation. Why might you want to place something farther away? If the person perceives something in a negative light, you can place it farther away. If the person perceives something in a positive light, you can place it closer to the person.

In addition, you can use the past tense to place the problem even farther away. Where in space do you visualize the following: "How *is that* a problem?" versus "How *was that* a problem?" You can say, "How *had that been* a problem?" to place it even farther away in the past.

When you want to create distance between an occurrence and a person, you can say

- "How did you perceive *that* in *that* way?"
- "When did *that* thought enter your mind?"

- "What were some of your thoughts and perceptions about *that?*"

When you want to put something closer to the person, you can say

- "By doing *this*, what are some of the benefits that you will reap?"
- "How might studying *this* material help you to achieve the many goals that you have for yourself?"
- "What are you noticing in terms of the benefits that you are receiving from spending time learning *this* information?"

Potential Functions for This Tip: Building Relationships, Teaching, Responding to Objections, Encouraging Students, Influencing Students, Resolving Conflicts

83. "The More You . . ., the more you . . ."

The more you intentionally focus on building students up, the more joy and satisfaction you gain as a teacher. The more you feel great about the work you are doing with students, the more you are motivated to have an even more powerful impact on their lives.

Linking two phrases together helps students believe that one causes the other: "The more you . . . the more you . . . ." Following are some examples:

- "*The more you* study, *the more you* increase your chances of doing well on the test."
- "*The more* times you attend class, *the more you* increase your chances of passing the class."
- "*The more you* participate in group activities in class, *the more you* build lasting relationships with your friends and colleagues."
- "*The more you* read on the topic, *the more you* can position yourself as a true expert in this area."
- "*The more you* incorporate feedback into your papers, *the more you* can grow as a writer."

- *"The more you* come to class with an excitement about learning everything that you possibly can, *the more you* can learn."

Potential Functions for This Tip: Teaching, Planning for the Future, Encouraging Students, Resolving Conflicts

84. "The Paper" Versus "Your Paper"

When you hear, "The paper is finished," where in space do you perceive it to be located? Where do you perceive it to be when you hear, "Your paper is finished"? Use "the" rather than "your" in sensitive conversations. If you are talking with a student about a paper and are giving feedback that the student could perceive to be negative, it is better to say "the paper" rather than "your paper." When you say "the paper," the student perceives the paper as being farther away. If you say "your paper," the student could interpret your feedback on the paper as being about him or her.

When you give positive feedback, feel free to say "your paper" or "your hard work on the paper" or "the work that you did." You want the student to associate your positive feedback with feeling good. Consider these examples of using "the paper" and "your paper":

- "What changes might be good to make to *the paper*?"
- "Here is some feedback on *the paper*."
- "What might be some ideas for refining *the paper*?"
- "I bet you are feeling really good about *your paper*!"
- "It looks like you worked hard on *your paper*."
- "*Your project* appears to be going really well!"

Potential Functions for This Tip: Teaching, Encouraging Students, Resolving Conflicts

85. "Think of Some Times When . . ."

We can consciously determine which learning states we want our students to experience. Do you want them to be curious or in a state of wild enthusiasm? Do you want them to want to discover everything they can discover, feel calm and serene, explore, have confidence, feel like experimenting, and feel joyful?

After you have decided which states would be beneficial for your students, you can demonstrate those states yourself so that your students will imitate you (Hall, 2004). Think of some times when you have been wildly enthusiastic about what you were teaching. What were some of the effects on your students? Think, too, of times when you have just felt "so-so" about what you were teaching. What impact did that state have on the students? We are unconsciously modeling and communicating states to our students every day. We might as well do it consciously.

Ask your students to think back in their lives and remember times when they were feeling certain ways, in order to help them have those feelings now. What might be some beneficial states for students to have in the classroom? You might want them to be curious, open to learning new things, excited about what they are learning, willing to delve into the material and discover new things, willing to use their creativity, willing to take risks, and so on. Of course, the intonation of your voice needs to match the state.

- *"Think of some situations* in which you were wildly enthusiastic. You were so excited that you couldn't wait to get started!"
- *"Think of some times* when you were experiencing a sense of discovery of new things. You wanted to explore and explore until you found out the answers to the things you wanted to know."
- *"Think of some times* when you were feeling extremely creative. Your mind was racing, and you were brainstorming many ideas. It seemed like you couldn't write down your ideas fast enough."

In order to assist your students in entering into these states, you can also tell stories about times when you were feeling particularly curious, excited about learning, enthusiastic about the content, and interested in discovering new things. By both inviting them to think about their lives and telling your own stories, you will ensure that they are in positive states and are ready to learn! What stories from your life related to various states would you like to share with students?

Potential Functions for This Tip: Teaching, Planning for the Future

86. Thoughts

Students are going to be involved in situations in which they have made wrong choices. Rather than giving them advice, punishing them, or telling them what we think they should do, we can put them in charge of the situation by sharing their thoughts. You might ask your students the following questions:

- "What are some of your *thoughts* about solving the situation?"
- "What are some of your *thoughts* about possibilities for moving forward?"
- "As you have been thinking about the progress that you are making, what are some of your *thoughts* about the reasons that you are progressing so rapidly toward your goals?"
- "Could you please share your *thoughts* about the strategies that you are using in the process of learning?"

Potential Functions for This Tip: Teaching, Planning for the Future, Responding to Objections, Encouraging Students, Influencing Students, Resolving Conflicts

87. "Type of Student Who . . ."

We can presuppose positive things about students by telling them positive things about themselves. How would you feel if someone came up to you and said, "You are the type of teacher who really cares about her class?" When we make statements such as these, we are helping students to develop positive identities:

- "You are the *type of student who* works hard to complete assignments, no matter the challenges."
- "You are the *type of person who* loves working toward goals and realizing his or her mission in life."
- "You are the *type of person who* cares deeply about social issues."
- "You are the *type of person who* has many friends."
- "You are the *kind of student who* completes your work on time and in a quality manner."

Potential Functions for This Tip: Building Relationships, Teaching, Planning for the Future, Responding to Objections, Encouraging Students, Influencing Students, Resolving Conflicts

88. Universal Experiences

People generally experience similar things. Most people remember what it was like to first learn the letters of the alphabet and to color. Most people remember what it was like to not enjoy a certain food or to sit down to a meal of their favorite foods. Most people remember what it was like to learn something new.

According to Hall (2004), we can invite students to remember these experiences in order to help them to begin feeling a certain way. States that we can invite them to remember include anticipation, joy, enthusiasm, experimentation, curiosity, exploration, discovery, and other emotions. We want to elicit states of confidence and help them to remember situations in the past that were perhaps somewhat like the situation in which they find themselves now. We want to help them realize that even if they initially had tentative feelings at the beginning of an experience in the past, they did well and learned, and they will do well and learn in this situation, too.

Some of the experiences that we can talk about with students include learning to write, entering school for the first time, wanting to buy something, liking certain types of food, realizing that a past belief is no longer true, or learning to do something. You might say, "You all remember what it was like to first learn the letters of the alphabet. You were perhaps a little bit timid at first, not knowing yet that you could learn them. Perhaps you worked hard at learning them. Perhaps you practiced them, and of course, you learned them! In addition, you had absolutely no idea of all the things just those 26 letters would open up to you and for you. There was no way for you to know at that time just how many opportunities and learnings just those 26 letters would bring to you! Learning _____ is a lot like learning the letters of the alphabet."

Another example: "Perhaps you remember your first day of school. You may have been a little hesitant to leave your familiar surroundings at first, yet you did, and as you did, you grew in confidence, didn't you? You met new friends, you formed many lasting friendships, and you learned more than you ever could have dreamed of learning. This class is a lot like that."

With older students, you might say, "You all remember what it was like when you were learning to drive. At first, perhaps, you were a little timid and not exactly sure about how it would turn out. You pressed the clutch down slowly, not sure what would happen. Perhaps it took some thought to remember to press the clutch down at the same time that you shifted gears, yet you learned how to do it, didn't you? Although you were a little tentative at first, soon you were driving with ease and confidence and couldn't believe that you ever wondered if you could do it without thinking. Learning these skills is a lot like that."

What are some of the feelings that we get when we hear each of these discussions? As we are telling the stories, it is important for us to demonstrate the state that we would like our students to have (i.e., curiosity, confidence, excitement, anticipation, enthusiasm, joy, etc.).

Potential Functions for This Tip: Teaching, Resolving Conflicts

89. "Us" and "We" Instead of "I" and "You"

The pronouns that we use can have a powerful impact on both our students and our colleagues. What impact do the following words have on your thinking?

- "*I* had him last year, *you* have him this year . . . good luck!"
- "*I* am going to do X. What are *you* going to do?"
- "*I* really like this. What do *you* like?"

What impact on thinking do the following questions using the pronouns, "we," "us," and "our" have?

- "How can *we* help Sarah to be successful?"
- "What might be some possible strategies that *we* can use in order to help all of *our* students do well on the upcoming tests?"
- "How can *we* all work together to make this an outstanding school program?"

In addition to using "us" and "we" with our colleagues in the school, we can use "us" and "we" when we are talking with students in our classrooms. By including ourselves along with the students, we can create a feeling of unity.

- "This really seems like it's fun for *us* to do."
- "*We* are working together cooperatively."
- "*We* are really enjoying working together toward accomplishing something that's fun for all of *us*!"

Potential Functions for This Tip: Building Relationships, Teaching, Encouraging Students, Influencing Students, Resolving Conflicts

90. Wait Time

Rowe (1986) emphasizes the importance of teachers using wait time. She found that, on average, teachers waited less than one second between asking a question and calling on a student to answer the question (wait time 1). She also found that teachers waited less than a second before asking another question after a student finished talking (wait time 2). In addition, she discovered that when teachers wait 2.7 or more seconds before calling on a student and before asking another question,

1. The length of student responses increases between 300% and 700%, in some cases more, depending on the study.

2. More inferences are supported by evidence and logical argument.

3. The incidence of speculative thinking increases.

4. The number of questions asked by students increases, and the number of experiments they propose increases.

5. Student-student exchanges increase; teacher-centered "show and tell" behavior decreases.

6. Failures to respond decrease.

7. Disciplinary moves decrease.

8. The variety of students participating voluntarily in discussions increases. Also, the number of unsolicited, but appropriate, contributions by students increases.

9. Student confidence, as reflected in fewer inflected responses, increases.

10. Achievement improves on written measures where the items are cognitively complex. (pp. 44–45)

Rowe also found that increased wait time led to powerful effects for teachers:

1. Teachers' responses exhibit greater flexibility. This is indicated by the occurrence of fewer discourse errors and greater continuity in the development of ideas.

2. The number and kind of questions asked by teachers changes.

3. Expectations for the performance of certain students seems to improve. (p. 45)

When I taught kindergarten, I read an article in which the authors said that short wait times actually teach students not to think. As a result, I began closing my eyes and counting—1,001, 1,002, 1,003, 1,004, 1,005—after asking each question. When I opened my eyes, most of the hands in the class would be up, and nearly all of the students would be eager to answer the question.

Potential Functions for This Tip: Building Relationships, Teaching, Planning for the Future, Responding to Objections, Encouraging Students, Influencing Students, Resolving Conflicts

91. "What Is . . ."

What is really wonderful about teaching is that we have numerous opportunities every day to affect countless lives, which will have incredible impacts for many years to come. By using the phrase "what is . . . ," we can imply a universal truth. Examples include the following:

- *"What is* so wonderful about working with you is that you work quickly and accurately."
- *"What is* absolutely fantastic about our class is that we can truly talk about things that come up."
- *"What is* fun in our class is that everyone enjoys being with each other."
- *"What is* really nice is that everyone in class works hard and contributes to the group discussion."
- *"What is* great about the way you are working is that you are really focusing on studying for the test."

Potential Functions for This Tip: Building Relationships, Teaching, Encouraging Students, Influencing Students

92. What, Why, and How

How often have we been asked to do things in a class with no idea why we were being asked to do them? I would have loved to have known the reason behind sitting in second grade with two strips of paper saying, "B says buh, buh, buh. C says cuh, cuh, cuh." I was bored out of my mind! Had I known the reason for doing these repetitions every day, I might have put more energy into what I was doing. Wellman and Lipton (2004) suggest that teachers and presenters follow the "what, why, and how" sequence (p. 13). First, say *what* you are going to be doing or covering. Then tell the group *why* they are going to be doing it. Then tell them *how* they are going to be doing it.

- "We are learning these rules so that you will be able to quickly and easily figure out new words when you encounter them in your reading. Here is how we will be doing it."
- "By taking these tests of the basic mathematics facts, you are learning to think quickly, as well as to internalize the facts that you will be using for the rest of your life. Here's how we will be going about it."
- "This chemistry principle will come in handy when you are cooking. Here is how we will be doing the experiment to demonstrate it. "

Potential Functions for This Tip: Teaching, Resolving Conflicts

93. "While . . ."

If I say, "While you read this book," what am I presupposing? I would be presupposing that you were reading this book and that something else was happening at the same time. We can use the word "while" to presuppose that students are doing what we requested. Following are some examples:

- *"While* you continue to complete your work, you may notice just how powerfully you are advancing toward your goals."
- *"While* you are studying, please keep in the back of your mind the many successes you are enjoying."
- *"While* you are working, I will be passing out the papers."
- *"While* you are reading, I will also be reading at my desk."
- *"While* we are walking to our next class, continue to think about possible solutions to the puzzle that we just presented."

Potential Functions for This Tip: Teaching, Planning for the Future, Encouraging Students, Influencing Students, Resolving Conflicts

94. "Will Today Be the Day That . . ."

We can create anticipation and eagerness about today in students by asking, "Will today be the day that . . . ?" This technique helps students to set expectations. Asking questions of students activates their thought processes, inviting them to come up with answers to the questions.

- *"Will today be the day that* you completely understand this concept?"
- *"Will today be the day that* you make the decision to get started on writing that paper in order to complete it long before it is due?"
- *"Will today be the day that* you are giving yourself positive encouragement about your ability to accomplish everything you ever dreamed of accomplishing?"
- *"Will today be the day that* you discover the piece that you hadn't yet learned that will transform the way you are thinking about this?"

Potential Functions for This Tip: Teaching, Planning for the Future, Responding to Objections, Encouraging Students, Influencing Students, Resolving Conflicts

95. Wondering

We can ask questions by wondering, a gentle way of inquiring. Schrumpf and colleagues (1997) recommend that peer mediators use the phrase "I'm wondering" as a way of asking questions.

- "I was *wondering* about what might have been happening."
- "I'm *wondering* about the thoughts behind the statement that you just made."
- "I'm *wondering* about what might be some possible solutions."

Potential Functions for This Tip: Teaching, Planning for the Future, Responding to Objections, Encouraging Students, Influencing Students, Resolving Conflicts

96. *Words That Change Minds*

Charvet's (1997) book *Words That Change Minds* talks about different ways that people operate in the world, called meta-programs. For example, some people like to move toward outcomes and goals, and other people like to move away from negative things. Other people put a combination of the two into practice. These preferences are neither right nor wrong; they are just the way people are, the way they view things, and the way they move in the world.

Another meta-program that Charvet discussed was sameness versus difference. Some people like for things to be the same, and others like for them to be different. When the "sameness" people are presented with something new, they like to compare it with what they already know and look for ways in which the new idea is the same as what they have experienced in the past. "Difference" people, on the other hand, like to examine new things based on how they are different from what they have experienced in the past.

In the early 1990s, when the standards-based curriculum movement was coming into the schools, one of my colleagues in administration came back to the building every day extremely discouraged. She lamented, "I tell the teachers about standards. Then they say,

'Oh, this is the same as what I have always done.' I do my best to show them how it is different, yet they insist on telling me how it is the same as what they have done in the past. We end up fighting about whether it is the same or different. I wish I didn't have to do this!"

My friend was working with teachers, many of whom, one could surmise from this brief story, were looking for the ways in which the new ideas were the same as what they already knew. They were not interested in finding out how this new method of teaching was different from what they were already doing. Charvet presents many other ways that people view the world and provides tips for language to use in order to build rapport with them and influence them in positive ways.

Potential Functions for This Tip: Building Relationships, Teaching, Planning for the Future, Responding to Objections, Encouraging Students, Influencing Students, Resolving Conflicts

97. "Yes"

Has anyone asked you a question for which the only answer was "Yes"? Salespeople capitalize on that. They ask us a number of questions for which the only answer that we can give is "Yes." Then, when we are in a "yes" mode, they invite us to buy what they are selling.

We can ask questions of students for which the answer is an obvious "yes" to help them get into the habit of agreeing with us (Hall, 2004). In order to answer "yes" to these questions, they must agree with what we are saying.

- "Have you already noticed just how much fun you are having as you learn valuable skills that you will be applying in many different contexts?"
- "Will you now recognize all of the possibilities that have already opened up to you and for you in the process of learning skills that will be valuable to you in a variety of areas?"

- "Are you curious to know just how much you are in the process of learning now?"
- "Have you yet noticed all of the applications that you are making in ways that will affect the world in wonderful and beneficial ways?"

Potential Functions for This Tip: Building Relationships, Teaching, Responding to Objections, Influencing Students, Resolving Conflicts

98. "Yet," "Until Now," "But Not for Long"

Tiny words like "yet," "until now," and "but not for long" can have great power. If a student says, "I can't do X," you could reply, "yet," "until now," or "but not for long" (Hall, 2006).

I had a lovely experience on a plane recently. The woman who sat next to me was doing sudoku. I had seen people doing the puzzles, yet I had never taken the time to learn to do them. She was extremely intent on what she was doing. When she paused, I asked her if she could please explain the process to me. She tore a page out of her book and, with a twinkle in her eyes, said, "The first page is free!"

As she gently led me along, asking me questions rather than telling me what to do, I thought, "She must be a teacher!" She led me to determine which numbers should go in which boxes. Sometimes she would say, "We can't know *yet*." Somehow, the way she said the word "yet" was reassuring. She had a lilt in her voice and a little bit of playfulness. With that tiny word, she seemed to be saying that it was OK, everything was fine, that was the way it was—even though we couldn't know *yet*, we would eventually know which number to write in the box.

I recently participated in a study group. The woman next to me didn't know the answer to something, and she said several times, in a demeaning voice, "I'm just dumb! I'm just plain dumb!" Basically, she was saying that her identity was a dumb person. I searched for something that I could say to encourage her and help her to see the situation differently. I said, "So . . . not knowing something *yet* means *dumb*?" She stopped, looked at me with a somewhat bewildered look, and then smiled, saying, "I guess not!"

I was talking with a friend who had a 5th grade son. She reported that recently, he had said, "Mom, I just can't learn this." She immediately responded, "Yet!" He stopped, gave a big smile, and quickly and easily accomplished what he had previously thought he could not do. Here are some examples for using these "little words" with your students:

- "I can't complete my homework."
- "*Yet.*"
- "I can't figure this out."
- "*But not for long.*"
- "I am confused."
- "*Until now.*"

After we have helped students to realize that they will be able to do it soon, we can ask questions such as the following:

- "What might be some of the next steps to take in the process of accomplishing this?"
- "What could be some resources on which you could draw in order to complete the project?"

Potential Functions for This Tip: Teaching, Planning for the Future, Responding to Objections, Encouraging Students, Influencing Students, Resolving Conflicts

99. "You First, Then Me"

We can ask students to do what they would like to do before doing what we would like them to do. We can acknowledge that students have things that they want to do in addition to the things that we want them to do. By linking them, we can imply that after they do what they want to do, they will automatically be doing what we want them to do.

- "Please have a fun time at recess *before* we start the new unit."
- "Please enjoy your lunch *before* we study for the spelling test."
- "Please talk with your friends for two minutes *before* opening your books to page 59."
- "Please enjoy talking with your friends on the bus *before* arriving at school ready to study."
- "Please take time with your family *before* coming to class."

Potential Functions for This Tip: Teaching, Influencing Students

100. Zeigarnik Effect

Zeigarnik discovered that when learners have uncompleted tasks, they tend to remember them and are motivated to continue thinking about them (as cited in Wlodkowski, 1986). Since we want to complete things, we have more tension around unfinished items. This is perhaps the reason that we wake up at night thinking about a task that we need to complete.

We can use the Zeigarnik effect to create a situation in which learners will continue thinking about what we have been discussing. We might ask a question for them to continue contemplating. We may leave a lesson unfinished and say that we will be discussing it more when we meet again. Consider the impact of the following statements:

- "We will be continuing our discussion of this topic tomorrow. Between now and then, please think about how you might apply these ideas in your personal and professional lives."
- "As you are leaving, please give thought to the possible causes behind what we are discussing. We will look forward to hearing your ideas during the next class."
- "Please be thinking of some possible applications for what you are learning to tell us at the next class session."

Potential Functions for This Tip: Teaching, Planning for the Future, Resolving Conflicts

Figure 1

100 Tips for Talking Effectively with Your Students

	Building Relationships	Teaching	Planning for the Future	Responding to Objections	Encouraging Students	Influencing Students	Resolving Conflicts
1. Acknowledging Learners' Current Experience	✓	✓	✓	✓	✓		✓
2. Adverbs	✓	✓	✓	✓	✓	✓	✓
3. "After . . ."		✓	✓	✓	✓	✓	✓
4. "And" or "Yet"—No "Buts"	✓	✓	✓	✓	✓	✓	✓
5. "As . . ."		✓	✓	✓	✓	✓	✓
6. "At This Time . . ."			✓	✓	✓	✓	✓
7. "Because" and "Since"		✓	✓	✓	✓	✓	✓
8. Becoming Someone Else			✓	✓	✓	✓	✓
9. "Before Friday" Instead of "By Friday"		✓	✓			✓	✓
10. "By Doing X . . ."		✓	✓	✓	✓	✓	✓
11. Can Do	✓	✓	✓	✓	✓	✓	✓
12. Choices	✓	✓	✓	✓	✓	✓	✓
13. Choosing To			✓	✓	✓		
14. Consciously Noticing				✓	✓	✓	✓
15. Contexts		✓		✓	✓	✓	✓
16. Continuing		✓	✓		✓		✓
17. Counterexamples				✓	✓	✓	✓
18. "Create for Yourself . . ."		✓	✓		✓	✓	✓
19. Curious		✓	✓	✓	✓	✓	✓
20. Denominalizing		✓	✓	✓	✓	✓	✓
21. Do It—Don't Try to Do It		✓	✓	✓	✓	✓	✓
22. "Don't . . . Unless You Really Want To . . ."		✓	✓	✓	✓	✓	✓
23. Eliminating "I"	✓	✓	✓	✓	✓	✓	✓

Figure 1

100 Tips for Talking Effectively with Your Students *(continued)*

	Building Relationships	Teaching	Planning for the Future	Responding to Objections	Encouraging Students	Influencing Students	Resolving Conflicts
24. Embedding Suggestions		✓		✓	✓	✓	✓
25. "Even Better"	✓	✓	✓	✓	✓	✓	✓
26. Feedback		✓			✓	✓	
27. Feeling Smart		✓			✓		
28. Flipping It				✓		✓	✓
29. Future Pacing		✓	✓	✓	✓	✓	✓
30. Green Elephants		✓	✓		✓	✓	✓
31. High Expectations	✓	✓	✓	✓	✓	✓	✓
32. "How . . . ?"		✓	✓	✓	✓	✓	✓
33. "I Apologize" Versus "I'm Sorry"				✓			✓
34. "I Will . . ."	✓	✓	✓			✓	✓
35. Identities	✓	✓	✓	✓	✓	✓	✓
36. Important Ideas		✓					
37. "In the Long Run"		✓	✓	✓	✓	✓	✓
38. "-ing" Words		✓	✓	✓	✓	✓	✓
39. Inquiring Rather Than Interrogating	✓	✓		✓			✓
40. Instructions		✓					
41. "It Is," "It Was"	✓	✓		✓	✓		
42. "It's Really About . . ."				✓	✓	✓	✓
43. "Know Best"	✓	✓	✓	✓	✓	✓	✓
44. Laughing	✓	✓	✓	✓	✓	✓	✓
45. Linking Learning with Students' Lives	✓	✓					
46. Long-Term Consequences of Actions			✓	✓	✓	✓	✓

Figure 1

100 Tips for Talking Effectively with Your Students *(continued)*

	Building Relationships	Teaching	Planning for the Future	Responding to Objections	Encouraging Students	Influencing Students	Resolving Conflicts
47. Magic Words	✓	✓				✓	✓
48. "Managing to . . ."				✓		✓	✓
49. Meanings				✓	✓	✓	✓
50. Metaphors	✓	✓	✓	✓	✓	✓	✓
51. Models of the World				✓		✓	✓
52. Naming Things Intentionally		✓				✓	
53. Networking Students	✓	✓	✓	✓	✓	✓	✓
54. Next Steps		✓	✓		✓	✓	✓
55. Not Tell You		✓		✓		✓	✓
56. "Noticed"	✓	✓		✓	✓	✓	
57. One-Liners				✓	✓	✓	
58. Owning Successes	✓	✓			✓		
59. Paraphrasing	✓	✓	✓	✓	✓	✓	✓
60. Past Tense		✓		✓	✓	✓	✓
61. Perceiving				✓		✓	✓
62. Planning		✓	✓		✓		✓
63. Pointing Out Growth		✓		✓	✓	✓	
64. Points of View		✓	✓	✓	✓		✓
65. Positive Words	✓	✓	✓	✓	✓	✓	✓
66. Pretending as Though You Can		✓	✓	✓	✓	✓	✓
67. Questions from Students	✓	✓					✓
68. Questions That Invite	✓	✓	✓	✓	✓	✓	✓
69. Refining Versus Improving	✓	✓			✓		

Figure 1

100 Tips for Talking Effectively with Your Students *(continued)*

	Building Relationships	Teaching	Planning for the Future	Responding to Objections	Encouraging Students	Influencing Students	Resolving Conflicts
70. Reframing		✓	✓	✓	✓	✓	✓
71. Resources		✓	✓	✓	✓	✓	✓
72. Review, Review, Review		✓					✓
73. "Say More About That"		✓	✓	✓			✓
74. Self-Assessing		✓					✓
75. "Someone Said . . ."	✓	✓	✓	✓	✓	✓	✓
76. Specifying	✓	✓	✓	✓	✓	✓	✓
77. "Stop And . . ."		✓		✓	✓	✓	✓
78. Strengths	✓	✓	✓	✓	✓	✓	✓
79. Student Names	✓	✓	✓	✓	✓	✓	✓
80. Systems Approach	✓	✓	✓	✓	✓	✓	✓
81. Tag Questions	✓	✓	✓	✓	✓	✓	✓
82. "That" Versus "This"	✓	✓		✓	✓	✓	✓
83. "The More You . . ., the more you . . ."		✓	✓		✓		✓
84. "The Paper" Versus "Your Paper"		✓			✓		✓
85. "Think of Some Times When . . ."		✓	✓				
86. Thoughts		✓	✓	✓	✓	✓	✓
87. "Type of Student Who . . ."	✓	✓	✓	✓	✓	✓	✓
88. Universal Experiences		✓					✓
89. "Us" and "We" Instead of "I" and "You"	✓	✓			✓	✓	✓
90. Wait Time	✓	✓	✓	✓	✓	✓	✓
91. "What Is . . ."	✓	✓			✓	✓	
92. What, Why, and How		✓					✓

Figure 1

100 Tips for Talking Effectively with Your Students *(continued)*

	Building Relationships	Teaching	Planning for the Future	Responding to Objections	Encouraging Students	Influencing Students	Resolving Conflicts
93. "While . . ."		✓	✓		✓	✓	✓
94. "Will Today Be the Day That . . ."		✓	✓	✓	✓	✓	✓
95. Wondering		✓	✓	✓	✓	✓	✓
96. *Words That Change Minds*	✓	✓	✓	✓	✓	✓	✓
97. "Yes"	✓	✓		✓		✓	✓
98. "Yet," "Until Now," "But Not for Long"		✓	✓	✓	✓	✓	✓
99. "You First, Then Me"		✓				✓	
100. Zeigarnik Effect		✓	✓				✓

References

Andreas, C. (1992). *Advanced language patterns: An advanced audio cassette program* [Audiotape and Transcript]. Boulder, CO: NLP Comprehensive.

Andreas, S., & Faulkner, C. (Eds.). (1994). *NLP: The new technology of achievement*. New York: Morrow.

Armor, D., Conroy-Oseguera, P., Cox, M., King, N., McDonnell, L., Pascal, A., et al. (1976). *Analysis of the School Preferred Reading Program in selected Los Angeles minority schools.* (Report No. R-2007-LAUSD). Santa Monica, CA: Rand Corporation.

Aronson, E. (1997, Spring). Review: Back to the future: Retrospective review of Leon Festinger's "A theory of cognitive dissonance." *The American Journal of Psychology, 110*(1), 127–137.

Asbell, H. C. (1983). Effects of reflection, probe, and predicate-matching on perceived counselor characteristics. *Dissertation Abstracts International, 44*(11), 3515B. (UMI No. AAT 8404790)

Aune, B. (2002). Teaching action research via distance. *Journal of Technology and Teacher Education, 10*(4), 461–479.

Bandler, R., & Grinder, J. (1979). *Frogs into princes: Neuro linguistic programming*. Moab, UT: Real People Press.

Bandler, R., & Grinder, J. (1982). *Reframing: Neuro-linguistic programming and the transformation of meaning*. Moab, UT: Real People Press.

Banyai, I. (1998). *Zoom*. London: Puffin.

Baskin, C. (2002). *Re-generating knowledge: Inclusive education and research.* Paper presented at the annual conference of the Canadian Indigenous and Native Studies Association (CINSA), Toronto, Ontario, Canada.

Bateson, G. (1972). *Steps to an ecology of mind: A revolutionary approach to man's understanding of himself*. New York: Ballantine Books.

Berliner, D. C. (1984). The half-full glass: A review of research on teaching. In P. L. Hosford (Ed.), *Using what we know about teaching* (pp. 51–77). Alexandria, VA: ASCD.

Brown, W. T., & Jones, J. M. (2004). The substance of things hoped for: A study of the future orientation, minority status perceptions, academic engagement, and academic performance of Black high school students. *Journal of Black Psychology, 30*(2), 248–273.

Bryant, D. P., Smith, D. D., & Bryant, B. R. (2008). *Teaching students with special needs in inclusive classrooms*. Boston: Pearson Education.

Charvet, S. R. (1997). *Words that change minds: Mastering the language of influence.* Dubuque, IA: Kendall/Hunt.

Cline, J. C. (1995). A correlation between what teachers know about adolescent characteristics and needs and how teachers behave as perceived by their students. *Dissertation Abstracts International, 56*(07), 2498A. (UMI No. 9538256)

Clyde, W., & Delohery, A. (2005). *Using technology in teaching*. New Haven, CT: Yale University Press.

Commission on the Whole Child. (2007). *The learning compact redefined: A call to action.* Alexandria, VA: ASCD.

Costa, A., & Garmston, R. (2002). *Cognitive Coaching: A foundation for Renaissance schools.* Norwood, MA: Christopher-Gordon.

Costa, A. L., & Garmston, R. J. (Revised by J. Ellison & C. Hayes). (2007). *Cognitive Coaching foundation seminar learning guide* (7th ed.). Highlands Ranch, CO: Center for Cognitive Coaching.

Costa, A. L., & Kallick, B. (Eds.). (2008). *Learning and leading with habits of mind: 16 essential characteristics for success.* Alexandria, VA: ASCD.

Cousins, N. (2005). *Anatomy of an illness as perceived by the patient.* New York: W. W. Norton & Company.

Curwin, R. L., Mendler, A. N., & Mendler, B. D. (2008). *Discipline with dignity: New challenges, new solutions* (3rd ed.). Alexandria, VA: ASCD.

Davis, B. M. (2007). *How to teach students who don't look like you: Culturally relevant teaching strategies.* Thousand Oaks, CA: Corwin.

Delgado-Gaitan, C. (2006). *Building culturally responsive classrooms: A guide for K–6 teachers.* Thousand Oaks, CA: Corwin.

Delgado-Gaitan, C. (2007). Fostering Latino parent involvement in the schools: Practices and partnerships. In S. J. Paik & H. J. Walberg (Eds.), *Narrowing the achievement gap: Strategies for educating Latino, Black, and Asian students* (pp. 17–32). New York: Springer.

Delpit, L. D. (1988). The silenced dialogue: Power and pedagogy in educating other people's children. *Harvard Educational Review, 58*(3), 280–298.

De Volder, M. L., & Lens, W. (1982). Academic achievement and future time perspective as a cognitive-motivational concept. *Journal of Personality and Social Psychology, 42*(3), 566–571.

Dilts, R. (1999). *Sleight of mouth: The magic of conversational belief change.* Capitola, CA: Meta Publications.

Dilts, T., & DeLozier, J. (2000). *Encyclopedia of systemic Neuro-Linguistic Programming and NLP new coding.* Scotts Valley, CA: NLP University Press.

Dreikurs, R., & Grey, L. (1968). *A new approach to discipline: Logical consequences.* New York: Hawthorn.

Edwards, J. L. (1993). The effect of Cognitive Coaching on the conceptual development and reflective teaching of first year teachers. *Dissertation Abstracts International, 54*(03), 895A. (UMI No. AAT 9320751)

Edwards, J. L., Ellison, J., Mitchell, L., & Thiru, Y. (2003). Cognitive Coaching online: Benefits and challenges. In J. Ellison & C. Hayes (Eds.), *Cognitive Coaching: Weaving threads of learning and change into the culture of an organization* (pp. 99–106). Norwood, MA: Christopher-Gordon.

Ellerbroek, W. C. (1978, Spring). Language, thought, & disease. *The CoEvolution Quarterly, 30*–38.

Ellison, J., Hayes, C., Costa, A., & Garmston, B. (2008). *Cognitive Coaching foundation seminar trainer's guide.* Highlands Ranch, CO: Center for Cognitive Coaching.

Evertson, C. M., & Weinstein, C. S. (Eds.). (2006). *Handbook of classroom management: Research, practice, and contemporary issues.* Mahwah, NJ: Lawrence Erlbaum.

Faulkner, C. (1991). *Metaphors of identity: Operating metaphors & iconic change* [Audiotape and booklet]. Lyons, CO: Genesis II.

Fay, J., & Funk, D. (1995). *Teaching with love and logic: Taking control of the classroom.* Golden, CO: The Love and Logic Press.

Feurestein, R. (2000). Mediated learning experience. In A. Costa (Ed.), *Teaching for intelligence II: A collection of articles* (pp. 275–284). Arlington Heights, IL: Skylight.

Flicker, E. S., & Hoffman, J. A. (2006). *Guiding children's behavior: Developmental discipline in the classroom.* New York: Teachers College Press.

Forsyth, S., Forbes, R., Scheitler, S., & Schwade, M. (1998). Talk during one-on-one interactions. *Primary Voices K–6, 7*(1), 9–15.

Gardner, H. (2006). *Multiple intelligences: New horizons in theory and practice.* New York: Basic Books.

Gay, G. (2000). *Culturally responsive teaching: Theory, research, and practice.* New York: Teachers College Press.

Gay, G. (2003). *Becoming multicultural educators: Personal journey toward professional agency.* San Francisco: Jossey-Bass.

Gilhooley, J., & Scheuch, N. S. (2000). *Using peer mediation in classrooms and schools: Strategies for teachers, counselors, and administrators.* Thousand Oaks, CA: Corwin.

Ginsberg, M. B. (2004). *Motivation matters: A workbook for school change.* San Francisco: Jossey-Bass.

Ginsberg, M. B., & Wlodkowski, R. J. (2000). *Creating highly motivating classrooms for all students: A schoolwide approach to powerful teaching with diverse learners.* San Francisco: Jossey-Bass.

Golden, S., Kist, W., Trehan, D. M., & Padak, N. (2005). A teacher's words are tremendously powerful: Stories from the GED Scholars Initiative. *Phi Delta Kappan, 87*(4), 311–315.

Grinder, M. (2000). *A healthy classroom: Educational group dynamics.* Battle Ground, WA: Michael Grinder and Associates.

Grinder, M. (2005). *ENVoY: Your personal guide to classroom management* (7th ed.). Vancouver, WA: Michael Grinder and Associates.

Grinder, M. (with Sayler, S., & Yenik, M.). (2009). *Charisma: The art of relationships* (3rd ed.). Battle Ground, WA: Michael Grinder & Associates.

Grinder, M. (with Yenik, M.). (2007). *The elusive obvious: The science of non-verbal communication.* Battle Ground, WA: Michael Grinder & Associates.

Hall, C. (2004). *The art of training.* Santa Cruz, CA: The NLP Connection.

Hall, C. (2006). *Language in action.* Santa Cruz, CA: The NLP Connection.

Hammer, A. L. (1983). Matching perceptual predicates: Effect on perceived empathy in a counseling analogue. *Journal of Counseling Psychology, 30*(2), 172–179.

Harvard Education Letter. (2008, January/February). Neither art nor accident: A conversation with Robert Pianta [Electronic version]. *Harvard Education Letter, 24*(1), 6–8. Retrieved September 3, 2008, from http://www.edletter.org/insights/pianta.shtml

Holcomb-McCoy, C. (2000). *Integrating multicultural perspectives in comprehensive guidance and counseling programs.* Paper presented at the annual conference of the American Counseling Association, Washington, DC.

Howard, S., & Johnson, B. (2000). What makes the difference? Children and teachers talk about resilient outcomes for children "at risk." *Educational Studies, 26*(3), 321–337.

Jackson, P. W. (1968). *Life in classrooms.* New York: Holt, Rinehart and Winston.

James, A. (2008). *School success for children with special needs: Everything you need to know to help your child learn.* San Francisco: Jossey-Bass.

Kilstein, H. D. (1993). Teacher perceptions of student responsiveness to therapeutic metaphor. *Dissertation Abstracts International, 54*(06), 2040A. (UMI No. AAT 9328603)

Kuykendall, J. (1993, Fall). "Please," "thank you," "you're welcome": Teacher language can positively impact prosocial development. *Day Care and Early Education, 21*(1), 30–32.

Laborde, G. Z. (1987). *Influencing with integrity: Management skills for communication & negotiation.* Palo Alto, CA: Syntony.

Ladson-Billings, G. (1994). *The dreamkeepers: Successful teachers of African American children.* San Francisco: Jossey-Bass.

Lakoff, G., & Johnson, J. (1980). *Metaphors we live by.* Chicago: University of Chicago Press.

Lambeth, C. R. (1980). Teacher invitations and effectiveness as reported by secondary students in Virginia. *Dissertation Abstracts International, 41*(05), 1923A. (UMI No. AAT 8024038)

Lee, S. J. (2007). The truth and myth of the model minority: The case of Hmong Americans. In S. J. Paik & H. J. Walberg (Eds.), *Narrowing the achievement gap: Strategies for educating Latino, Black, and Asian students* (pp. 171–184). New York: Springer.

Maldonado Torres, S. E. (2008). Identifying Latinos' learning styles and demographic factors to support their learning performance. *Dissertation Abstracts International, 70* (03), A. (UMI No. AAT 3350588).

Marzano, R. J. (with Marzano, J. S., & Pickering, D. J.) (2003). *Classroom management that works: Research-based strategies for every teacher.* Alexandria, VA: ASCD.

McCarthey, S. J. (1994). Students' understanding of metaphors in teachers' talk about writing. *Language Arts, 71*(8), 598–605.

McCombs, B. L., & Whisler, J. S. (1997). *The learner-centered classroom and school: Strategies for increasing student motivation and achievement.* San Francisco: Jossey-Bass.

McGee-Cooper, A. (1992). *You don't have to go home from work exhausted: A program to bring joy, energy, and balance to your life.* New York: Bantam.

McGee-Cooper, A. (1993). *Time management for unmanageable people: The guilt-free way to organize, energize, and maximize your life.* New York: Bantam.

Meyer, W. U., Bachmann, M., Biermann, U., Hempelmann, M., Plöger, F. O., & Spiller, H. (1979). The informational value of evaluative behavior: Influences of praise and blame on perceptions of ability. *Journal of Educational Psychology, 71*(2), 259–268.

Montgomery, K. J. (2007). Investigations of the mirror neuron system using functional MRI. *Dissertation Abstracts International, 68*(03), B. (UMI No. 3256580).

Newman, E. J. (1993). The effect of teacher efficacy, locus-of-control, and teacher enthusiasm on student on-task behavior and achievement. *Dissertation Abstracts International, 54*(07), 2516A. (UMI No. 9334264)

O'Connor, J., & Seymour, J. (1990). *Introducing Neuro-Linguistic Programming: Psychological skills for understanding and influencing people* (Rev. ed.). San Francisco: Aquarian Press.

Paik, S. J. (2007). Conclusion and recommendations. In S. J. Paik & H. J. Walberg (Eds.), *Narrowing the achievement gap: Strategies for educating Latino, Black, and Asian students* (pp. 185–193). New York: Springer.

Prusak, K. A., Vincent, S. D., & Pangrazi, R. P. (2005). Teacher talk. *Journal of Physical Education, Recreation and Dance, 76*(5), 21–25.

Purkey, W. W. (2000). *What students say to themselves: Internal dialogue and school success.* Thousand Oaks, CA: Corwin Press.

Purkey, W. W. (2006). *Teaching class clowns (and what they can teach us).* Thousand Oaks, CA: Corwin.

Purkey, W. W., & Novak, J. M. (1996). *Inviting school success: A self-concept approach to teaching, learning, and democratic practice* (3rd ed.). Belmont, CA: Wadsworth.

Ream, R. K., & Stanton-Salazar, R. D. (2007). The mobility/social capital dynamic: Understanding Mexican American families and students. In S. J. Paik & H. J. Walberg (Eds.), *Narrowing the achievement gap: Strategies for educating Latino, Black, and Asian students* (pp. 67–89). New York: Springer.

Richardson, J. (1987). *The magic of rapport: How you can gain personal power in any situation.* Capitola, CA: Meta Publications.

Rong, X. L., & Brown, F. (2007). Educational attainment of immigrant and non-immigrant young Blacks. In S. J. Paik & H. J. Walberg (Eds.), *Narrowing the achievement gap: Strategies for educating Latino, Black, and Asian students* (pp. 91–107). New York: Springer.

Rosenthal, R., & Jacobson, L. (1992). *Pygmalion in the classroom: Teacher expectations and pupils' intellectual development.* Norwalk, CT: Crown House Publishing.

Rowe, M. B. (1986). Wait time: Slowing down may be a way of speeding up. *Journal of Teacher Education, 37*(1), 42–49.

Rowe, R. W. (1998). Examining teacher talk: Revealing hidden boundaries for curricular change. *Language Arts, 75*(2), 103–107.

Schrumpf, F., Crawford, D. K., & Bodine, R. J. (1997). *Peer mediation: Conflict resolution in schools—Program guide* (Rev. ed.). Champaign, IL: Research Press.

Short, K., Kaufman, G., Kaser, S., Kahn, L. H., & Crawford, K. M. (1999). "Teacher-watching": Examining teacher talk in literature circles. *Language Arts, 76*(5), 377–385.

Siu-Runyan, Y. (2001). Teacher talk: Developing voice and choice in writing. *School Talk, 6*(2), 2–4.

Stouthard, M. E. A., & Peetsma, T. T. D. (1999). Future-time perspective: Analysis of a facet-designed questionnaire. *European Journal of Psychological Assessment, 15*(2), 99–105.

Teolis, B. (2002). *Ready-to-use conflict-resolution activities for elementary students.* San Francisco: Jossey-Bass.

Thompson, G. L. (2007). Improving the schooling experiences of African American students: What school leaders and teachers can do. In S. J. Paik & H. J. Walberg (Eds.), *Narrowing the achievement gap: Strategies for educating Latino, Black, and Asian students* (pp. 153–170). New York: Springer.

Tracz, S. M., & Gibson, S. (1986, November). *Effects of efficacy on academic achievement.* Paper presented at the annual meeting of the California Educational Research Association, Marina del Rey, CA.

Wanzer, M. B., & Frymier, A. B. (1999). The relationship between student perceptions of instructor humor and students' reports of learning. *Communication Education, 48,* 48–62.

Warlick, D. F. (2007). *Classroom blogging: A teacher's guide to blogs, wikis, & other tools that are shaping a new information landscape* (2nd ed.). Raleigh, NC: The Landmark Project.

Waxman, H. C., Padrón, Y. N., & García, A. (2007). Educational issues and effective practices for Hispanic students. In S. J. Paik & H. J. Walberg (Eds.), *Narrowing the achievement gap: Strategies for educating Latino, Black, and Asian students* (pp. 131–151). New York: Springer.

Wellman, B., & Lipton, L. (2004). *Data-driven dialogue: A facilitator's guide to collaborative inquiry.* Sherman, CT: MiraVia.

Werner, E. E. (1989). Children of the garden island. *Scientific American, 260*(4), 106–111.

Wlodkowski, R. J. (1984). *Motivation and teaching: A practical guide.* Washington, DC: National Education Association.

Wlodkowski, R. J. (1986). *Enhancing adult motivation to learn.* San Francisco: Jossey-Bass.

Wlodkowski, R. J., & Ginsberg, M. B. (1995). *Diversity and motivation: Culturally responsive teaching.* San Francisco: Jossey-Bass.

Wlodkowski, R. J., & Jaynes, J. H. (1990). *Eager to learn: Helping children become motivated and love learning.* San Francisco: Jossey-Bass.

Yapko, M. D. (1980). Neuro-linguistic programming, hypnosis, and interpersonal influence. *Dissertation Abstracts International, 41*(08), 3204B. (UMI No. AAT 8103393)

Zhou, M. (2007). Divergent origins and destinies: Children of Asian immigrants. In S. J. Paik & H. J. Walberg (Eds.), *Narrowing the achievement gap: Strategies for educating Latino, Black, and Asian students* (pp. 109–128). New York: Springer.

Index

judgments, as feedback, 68–69

key questions, 7–9
kinesthetic words, 17
"know best", 90

language
    in building relationships, x, 39
    childhood development and, ix–x
    in communicating high expectations,
        xviii–xix, 77
    in establishing rapport, 15–17
    teaching effectiveness and, 40
    thinking and, x
large projects, dividing into smaller tasks,
    124, 135
Latino students, 36
laughing, 91
learning, metaphors for, 13
learning states, promoting desired,
    138–140
Lewis, Ann, 6, 92
life, metaphors for, 11–12
long-term consequences, 92–93
long-term planning, 40–41

magic words, 94–95
"managing to . . .", 95
Massively Multiplayer Online Role-Playing
    Games (MMORPGs), 29–30
meanings, 96
mediation of conflicts, 43–45, 153–157f
metaphors, 11–13, 97–98
meta-programs, 148–149
mirroring, in establishing rapport, 13–14
mirror neuron system, 13–14
misbehavior, systems approach to reasons
    for, 134–135
mission, 81
MMORPGs (Massively Multiplayer Online
    Role-Playing Games), 29–30
modeling communication skills, xxi
models of the world, 98–99
multicultural interactions. *See* culturally
    diverse students
Multiuser Virtual Environments (MUVEs),
    29–30

names, of students, 132–133
naming things intentionally, 99–100
Native American students, 33, 36
negative language, xviii, 55–56, 75–76, 114

networking students, 100–101
Neuro-Logical Levels, 81–84
new topics, introducing, 70–71
next steps, 101–102
Nicenet, 28
Nonverbal Classroom Management, xxi
nonverbal communication
    approachable vs. credible voice in,
        18–19, 117–118
    in asking for questions from students,
        116
    in communicating high expectations,
        77
    with culturally diverse students, 34
    in establishing rapport, 14–15
    in inquiring vs. interrogating, 87
note writing, 23–24
"noticed", 103
"not tell you", 102–103

objections, responding to, 41–42,
    153–157f
one-liners, 103–104
online bulletin boards, 28
online environment, application of lan-
    guage tips to, 37–38
open-ended questions, 87, 120
owning successes, 104–105

paraphrasing, 105–107
parent interactions, 23–25
Partners in Rhyme, 30
passing time, 99
past tense, in stating problems, 107–108
perceptions, altering, xxi–xxii, 108–109
personal information, as feedback, 69
phone calls, 24–25
planning
    dividing tasks into doable segments,
        110–111
    for the future, 40–41, 153–157f
Plato, xix
"please", 94–95
plurals, in asking questions, 118
podcasting, 30
Podomatic, 30
pointed questions, 87
pointing out growth, 111–112
points of view, 112–113
positive attitude, 1–4, 55–56
positive intentions, 9–11
positive language, 55–56, 75–76, 114–115

About the Author

Jenny Edwards, PhD, has been working in the field of education for 35 years and has taught at the elementary, middle school, and university levels. In addition, she served in staff development in Jefferson County Schools in Denver, Colorado, for four years and was involved in mentoring first- and second-year teachers and presenting seminars. She earned a Bachelor of Science degree in elementary education from the University of Tennessee at Knoxville (UTK), specializing in early childhood education; a Master of Science degree in elementary education from UTK, specializing in reading; and a doctorate in human and organizational systems from Fielding Graduate University in Santa Barbara, California. She has been studying the impact of words on thinking patterns since the early 1990s.

Presently, Jenny is teaching doctoral students in the School of Educational Leadership and Change at Fielding Graduate University in Santa Barbara. She also leads seminars on Cognitive Coaching, Adaptive Schools, Callahan's Thought Field Therapy, and other topics around the world. She has presented on these topics in French, Spanish, Italian, and English in 11 countries.

Jenny can be reached by e-mail at jedwards@fielding.edu.